RESPECT THE MIC

CELEBRATING 20 YEARS OF POETRY FROM A CHICAGOLAND HIGH SCHOOL

EDITED BY

HANIF ABDURRAQIB **FRANNY CHOI** **PETER KAHN** **DAN "SULLY" SULLIVAN**

FOREWORD BY TYEHIMBA JESS

PENGUIN WORKSHOP

T0005134

**In memory of Ishma Stewart, Beth Cheney,
Daniel Escalona, and Dylan Thorn. You left us
too soon, but your impact resonates.**

W

PENGUIN WORKSHOP
An imprint of Penguin Random House LLC, New York

First published in the United States of America by Penguin Workshop,
an imprint of Penguin Random House LLC, New York, 2022

This paperback edition published by Penguin Workshop,
an imprint of Penguin Random House LLC, New York, 2023

Owing to limitations of space, credit for individual
poems and essays can be found beginning on page 169.

Collection copyright © 2022 by Hanif Abdurraqib,
Franny Choi, Peter Kahn, and Daniel Sullivan
Illustrations copyright © 2022 by Timba Smits

Visit us online at penguinrandomhouse.com.

Library of Congress Control Number: 2022930931

Printed in the United States of America

ISBN 9780593226827

2nd Printing

LSCC

CONTENTS

MONSTERS AT HOME

WELCOMES, FAREWELLS, AND ODES

SURVIVAL TACTICS

ONCE A POET

When I first opened the pages of *Respect the Mic*, I couldn't help but reflect on the many classrooms, community centers, and prisons that I had the privilege of teaching in during my years in Chicago, a place I grew up in for eighteen years, growing through stumbles and starts into where I am today, eighteen years later (!), still stumbling and starting my way through line after line after line of poetry. It was in those classrooms—the Gallery 37 spaces, open mics, slams, HotHouse, Guild Complex, Young Chicago Authors, Oak Park and River Forest High School [OPRFHS], Green Mill, Spices, and many other spaces—that I was able to better hear how to put the world on the page. Letter by letter, the streets and alleys, the bitter-cold winters and blazing summers wrote their poems into me with the asphalt and blues bars singing their sweltered up names onto mine.

When you read these poems, you will no doubt hear the true voice of Chicagoland for yourself, the collusion of city and suburb, alley and lawn, that make up the capital of the Midwest. You will hear echoes of the great brawling, butchering, kitchenette-historied, Gold Coast–glittered blues town. You'll feel the bass line of house music, the thrum of trap, the chorus of Cumbia. The great thing about coming of age as a writer in Chicago is that you have a skyscrapered, schoolyarded, L train–tracked electricity in each space you sprawl into—a checkerboard of ethnicities to navigate and explore all the American tongues. In Chicagoland, poets inhabit the XY axes of gridded streets to teach you that if the poem is gonna be worth it, it better sneak sweat-close to your skin and snatch off your chains. It better out-howl the Hawkish wind pushing down Michigan Avenue midwinters. It better be as scrawny-legged graceful as the grade-school hoopers in the park after dark. It better grin lopsided with a gold-toothed glint before it spits out a trochee or an iamb.

OPRFHS has been an intrepid safe house for poetry over the past three decades. It is home to a cadre of extraordinary teachers with an extraordinary interest in bringing poets from all over the country to their auditorium, filling the stage with verse after verse, book after book, in front of a packed audience of young listeners entranced with the power of The Word.

On that stage, and in these pages, you will also hear how a poet "can't wait for the day where I find out who I wanna be . . ." you will understand even further why "she was the only one brave enough / to say it out loud." You'll hear bullets in bucket hats, an opus of bucket drums, and a baile on a Friday night. This collection is a bit of a reunion—a calling of voices that have been shaped and billowed and baked in the sun of each other's voices, each other's shouts in the hallways and classrooms of this Respect for The Mic. 'Cause that is what it boils down to in the end. Respect. That's all we really have left, and when it's done right, that's all you really need to lean on. This OPRFHS literary tradition is a luscious, living, lie-killing, life-dealing part of doing it right. Inclusive, expansive, and digging into the well of American identity in all its myriad possibilities toward a More Human World. Drinking from the heart of the heart of a city that's got a Mississippi train track querying through its Music:

What city were you born in? A conditional war zone—a consequence of blessings.

I digress. The point is that this is supposed to be a foreword. But once you in it, you be all the way in it. And that's all the forward you need to make it back Home again. You'll see what I mean. You'll hear it, too, those voices in the hall . . .

In conclusion, I leave you with two phrase poems I learned in Chicago: the salutations of Kwame Nkrumah and the mighty Association for the Advancement of Creative Musicians . . .

Forward Ever, Backward Never!   ***   Ancient to the Future!

—**Tyehimba Jess**

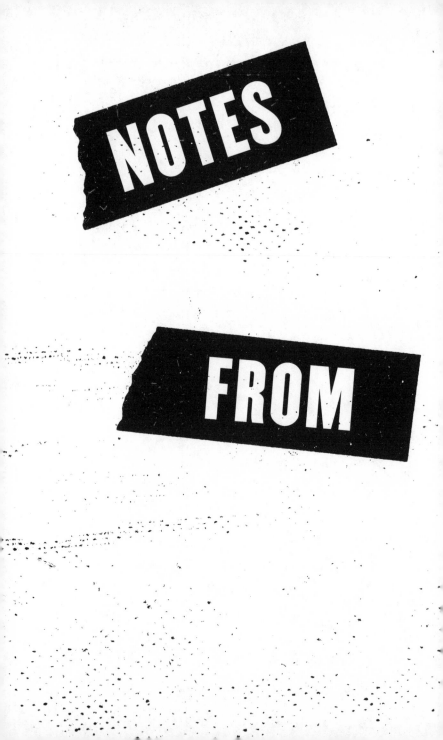

NOTES

FROM

When I became a public high school English teacher in Oak Park in 1994, I was terrified of teaching poetry. Poetry felt like a riddle I could never solve. How could I teach something that I myself didn't understand? I muddled my way through with the poems I had been taught in high school, the very ones that made me hate it because they made me feel stupid and I couldn't see myself in them. In 1998, I brought in a former student, Jonathan Vaughn, to rescue my poetry unit. I watched my students' faces wake up as he connected music lyrics to poetry, explained that "rap" stands for Rhythm And Poetry, told them about poetry slams, and encouraged them to write and share their own poems. Imagine that! I was embarrassed and inspired at the same time. "Can we have a poetry slam, Mr. Kahn?" the students rang out. And we did. A week later, the student with the lowest grade in the class came out on top with a rap about his writing pad that he took with him everywhere. "Brandon, where the hell have you been hiding that!" was a song lyric that we all sang out together. This is when poetry transformed from enemy to ally.

The next year, I redesigned my approach to poetry with a focus on contemporary poets like Patricia Smith and Saul Williams, who wrote about topics my students could relate to and engage with. (Patricia was the first poet I ever brought to my classroom.) I also started thinking more about what was then called the racial "achievement gap" and is now more aptly called the "opportunity gap." It has been a horribly resilient problem that has existed at our school since I started teaching there. This gap includes roughly a one point difference in weighted grade point average between white and Black students. And I thought one way to combat this rift was to create what is now called the Oak Park and River Forest Spoken Word Club.

We wanted the club to create a place of belonging for all our members, and particularly our Black students, where their experiences and voices could be heard loudly, proudly, and clearly. Each week, we celebrate our "study table all-stars" (those earning good grades) with snaps and cheers, while holding accountable and encouraging those with low grades. Students have set up peer-to-peer tutoring, and captains take pride when everyone in their group is an all-star. We teach writing craft, too, so students can see and show off their talent. So their words can resonate on the page, as well as the stage.

The Spoken Word club was conceived in large part because of students like Dan "Sully" Sullivan. Sully had the lowest grade in my class when I first met him. But before I knew it, he went from planning to drop out of high school on his seventeenth birthday to starring in our newly created Spoken Word Club. That is the beauty of the club: It has created a space to give students, like Brandon and Sully, a place to call their own, a place to belong. It also gave them a reason to show up to school in the first place.

Sully's parents told me on several occasions that poetry "saved his life." Poetry saved me in a way, too. It saved my career and changed the trajectory of my life. Teaching can be a draining profession, and I nearly abandoned it. But watching a community and its future leaders develop right in front of your eyes is an amazing thing. Seeing students who didn't believe in themselves win national poetry prizes or earn full tuition college scholarships is like watching a magic trick: I'm still guessing at the secret behind it.

At the Oak Park and River Forest Spoken Word Club, we've built a legacy where rookies eventually become captains and where graduates come back to work with us. Because poetry is the starting blocks, the finish line, and most importantly, the baton. In Spoken Word Club, the phrase "respect the mic" reigns supreme. Our student leaders shout it out like an order if anyone dares to talk when someone is reciting a poem. It's a call of pride and history and tradition and hope. Respect the mic—you have the floor.

—**Peter Kahn**

꜀ᙏᙏᙏ

Peter is right. I was an apathetic student. It wasn't that I was a bad kid. I just didn't like to do things like, you know, homework. It wasn't my parents. I came from a supportive home. I'm lucky in that way. Apathy was a privilege and one I chose to exercise freely. It wasn't even that I didn't like school. I was searching for a place where I felt like myself, was accepted for everything that I am and was witnessed. I found that in the Spoken Word Club.

My senior year, I wrote a collaborative poem with fellow club member Michael Pogue for a poetry showcase at the school. We titled it "Meditation" and, though it was far from a quiet mantra, it was rhythmic and guttural, a battle cry to find peace in ourselves amongst the chaos of high school. "I only see clearly by closing my eyes then tap into a continuum of clarity / Very rarely do people bury barriers carefully." Young adults, especially young men, are conditioned to build a fortress around their emotions as a method of survival.

Mike and I, through poetry and the club, began to learn how to break through the gates of the fortress. We had notebooks in hand while we dangled our legs over the large stone wall at Scoville Park and laughed while we watched the blur of suburban traffic. We talked for hours and worked to record it all in ink. We wrote poems for our fathers and prayers for our future selves. We'd practice in front of storefront windows so that we could see the reflection of our gestures and plot our stage points. We'd spend hours in an empty classroom after school to get feedback from Mr. Kahn. My friendship with Mike helped me develop a vulnerability and willingness to deepen my connections to others. This is what the Spoken Word Club gifted me. It opened me up to more than just a new way of learning, but also a new way of being in and interacting with the world around me.

In terms of the club's success, there is an X factor beyond the poetry and its built-in community. At the heart of the program, there is Peter Kahn. When I was a junior in high school, he found me sleeping through class and searched for a way to reach me. It's why so many of us have found a home in spoken word. It wasn't just poetry that saved my life, it was a teacher who took the time to recognize that poetry has power, and he's now helped generations of young people harness it, break through their own fortresses, and find a home in themselves.

I often joke that I was in high school for seventeen years. I spent thirteen years after graduating as cosponsor of the Spoken Word Club alongside Peter. Since high school, I have read poems, performed, and taught creative writing classes and workshops all around the world. I've received master's degrees in poetry and English, and made appearances on HBO and NPR. None of this would have been possible without the Spoken Word Club. Not only because of what it taught me about poetry, but because of what it taught me about leadership, mentorship, collaboration, and friendship. The first time I taught poetry in a classroom at OPRFHS, I sweated through my Ecko polo shirt. I was bewildered, but I have learned bewilderment is the point at which all poems start. We dislodge from the immediate circumstances of our lives and discover something new there.

I am proud to say that my life as a student—befriending my bewilderment, making sense of and articulating my inner-world, learning to let people past the fortress, and then helping them through theirs—hasn't been a lonely experience. It is one that so many other students have lived and are living out after joining the Oak Park River Forest High School Spoken Word Club. Though each of the poems in this anthology are events unto themselves, they open up to a larger sphere of community, one that lets us all in through the front gate. This book is a breathing testament to what happens when we truly listen to each other and celebrate how it sounds when individual voices speak up in unison.

—Dan "Sully" Sullivan

~*~

We are so proud of the seventy-six poets in this anthology, some of whom are still in high school, others who haven't put pen to paper in years, and others who have made careers of writing. They represent just a small percentage of those from our club who have been transformed by poetry. We welcome you to our home, where we've been poetically sharing our stories since 1999.

—Peter Kahn and Dan "Sully" Sullivan

Dan "Sully" Sullivan (OPRFHS class of 2000. Original Spoken Word Club member. BA in poetry—Columbia College. MFA in creative writing and MA in English language and literature—Indiana University. Higher education administrator. Poetry educator. Father of two.)

& I Can Find A Home There, Too.

When mom lost some of her hearing, the noise of traffic & city
buses at the curb out front drove forward from the backdrop

of our minds & pulled up at our dinner table in Brighton Park,
house on the corner of 42nd & California. I went to Peace

Lutheran for kindergarten & missed the crossing guard when
she was hospitalized after a hit & run. We moved to Oak Park,

first suburb west of the city. It was a lot closer to downtown
but that city limit spoke volumes. In the fifties, they built cul-de-

sacs all down Austin Ave at the edge of town. It was less about
holding & more about keeping out. Ludacris & Hemingway both

went to my high school. I guess I'm asking who gets to speak
for the city. I lived in Chicago more years than anywhere else

but what is mine to hold, if anything. Maybe I thought I was
part of the landscape. Some urban pastoral romance that connected

me to place. Where am I even from. Rakim said, *it ain't where
you from, it's where you at* & Edward Sharpe said, *home is wherever*

I'm with you. Our CD player doesn't work so Whitney & I flip radio
stations a lot when driving between Illinois & Indiana. I lean more

toward a Rakim ethos. I don't even think Edward Sharpe is
one person but I do think he's white. So what truth can I live in.

Chicago was never mine. That doesn't mean I can't love it.
It does mean I can leave. It means there is another landscape

& I can find a home there, too.

Kyla Robateau (OPRFHS class of 2021.)

Identity, Black

My whole life, I seemed to forget my identity, Black.
Only moved to Oak Park because it's diverse, Black.
Too light skinned to be my father's daughter, Black,
with hair too knotted to be my mom's kin, Black.
In Naperville on the entire street it was just us, Black,
and in elementary school it was only me, Black.
When my dad came to pick me up, a child screamed, Black,
a color she had never seen was a miscreation, and Black,
a little me, transferred schools to see people with tinted skin, Black,
where the grades were lower and they couldn't afford books because Black,
had no money and no knowledge. Lived in a neighborhood where Black,
the n-word, made its voyage to my dad behind my back, because Black,
shouldn't be making more money than the white kids' parents. So later me,
Black,
and my brother moved to Oak Park, without having to suffer hate for Black.
On Halloween night one year later, I went out with a friend,
Black, only to find torment from a neighbor thinking we, Black,
couldn't possibly live in this neighborhood. As the night pressed on,
Black,
I slept, and couldn't not find any explanation to the hate, hard Black.

Asia Calcagno (OPRFHS class of 2010. Two-time Louder Than a Bomb [LTAB] member. Recipient of the Posse Scholarship. BA in English and language arts—Connecticut College. MFA in creative writing—Bennington College. Former high school English teacher. Director of programs— 826Chi.)

Password Security Questions Ask Me the Right Questions to Know I Am Always Afraid

What is your mother's maiden name? Name she refused to keep.

A throat-stabbing bone. Another cave in her stomach. Name anchored
to her feet and wings threaded through the back. Call her old name a stack
of mail

on a dead mother's table which whispers, "Come home you
nameless fool." *What is your father's middle name?* A shovel and spade
cracking against rock. Some name I know but wish I didn't. Who I dare
call him. Who I dare speak. Supposedly biblical. I suppose a saint. A son
of someone. A son of a gun. The carpenter who built a wooden child
he couldn't

upkeep. *What city were you born in?* A conditional war zone—a consequence
of blessings. The place where I bleed and hose myself bloodless in
my front

yard. City where women who ride trains place pretty razors under a tongue
and buoy their heart above water. *On what street did you grow up?*
The corner of Austin and Chicago. The corner of Madison and Menard.
The vacant lot of Trumbull and Franklin. Always down the street from
a corner

store. A block from the garden house. Eyeshot from men who wave and wink
from laundromats, barber shop windows, and Food & Liquors. Where
I bust his

head clean open like a coconut and call it my defense. I guess a place where
the wind teaches

me how to pack and go. *What does your name mean?* Sunrise. East.
I imagine

the sun orbits my earth. I imagine everyone calls me the truth and not a lie.
    If we're on the block, they think I mean Honey. Baby. Red. Stubborn.
    My mama

calls me sugar but my daddy calls me nothing. Call me a child in every one
of my years
    with small fists wrapped around my father's first drink. In a dream, I
    find myself

standing alone in a blizzard with mean wind blowing into my ears. I echo:
What do you call
    your life? I answer to myself: something special. The one I'm always
    running from.

Matthew Minich (OPRFHS class of 2019. College student—James Madison University. Eagle Scout.)

Softball on County-T

straight beyond the overgrown baseball field
the long slender hair of the earth still grows and twists toward the sky
unkempt grass covered by a dusting of coarse sand
beat in the leather of the mitt and smell the varnish
the only thing that evades me is the thrill of the game
I can picture the hot dogs—Chicago style
celery salt and relish pushing up against sports pepper
the white chalk chipped into the black slate of scoreboard
a quick run down County Road 'T'
but we couldn't forget softballs or the bat
or the speaker and microphone
our sweat soaking into every dry wood beam of bleacher
empty plastic bottles run dry as the sun ran hot
crickets and lightning bugs came out as the day began to close
hugs and handshakes peppered the grass
I wish I could have played
through the night

Kyla Pereles (OPRFHS class of 2021. Gold Key & National American Voices Medal Nominee—Scholastic Art & Writing Awards. College student—Grinnell College. Four-time LTAB member.)

Oak Park Mutters Statistics

A website stutters numbers
about my town sheepishly
pushing them all the way
to the bottom

The percentage of residents living in poverty—8.5%
Then the parentheses:
(6% for white residents)
(9.6% for Hispanic residents)
(14.3% for Black residents)

I wonder why it is only the poverty statistic
that mentions race
Then I remember everything is about money
That in this cushy suburb racial bias loves to glare
back at you from the inside of a wallet

In this chunk of non-city
the people are proud
of their diversity
Even as the achievement
gap at my high school
glares at them

Back when the *Chicago Tribune* covered
the 1919 Chicago riots
they were overshadowed

by the streetcar strike which
inconvenienced white
people who had to find
other ways to get to work
I bet no Oak Park wife
looked toward the lake
and saw Black bodies

I wonder how many of their
children have done anything
other than cast problems under bottom lips
letting injustice sit with stale breath
Their "hate has no home here" lawn signs
resting in freshly trimmed grass
I can feel them eyeing me
questioning if I belong here
as I walk past

I think about pulling all the signs out
Telling my neighbors to learn their own statistics
Will they see me in parentheses?

A part of me hopes they don't
Is this why I straighten my hair
for every school picture?
So for those few minutes before class,
a teacher may see me as something
other than Latina
Is Oak Park the cut lawn
and the sign planted in it
or white women
standing proud behind their liberal yard signs?

Where does it fit in a world that would rather focus
on anything but the problems across the street?

I just hope that when Oak Park makes its choice
it will say it without muttering

Matthew Buchta (OPRFHS class of 2020. Skateboarder.)

Puerto Rican leather sits on my shoulders

Puerto Rican leather sits on my shoulders
Balanced like wooden bats we swing in summer.
"Come on, Cin. Give me the boy. We're gonna go watch the game."
The crack of wood against cowhide and cork.
Sweat drips like gutters in a summer gale.
Grandfather left his story in my hands but dropped off
this world before I could tell it.
Puerto Rico was his prison. America, his diamond.
I hit first base, a sewer cap in the middle of the 900 block of Mapleton.
Dirt roads and brick stitched his game.
Pecked my forehead with dry lips. "Nieto," he would whisper.
A baseball-size hole spliced its way through a glass door.
But all that could be heard were summer crickets singing.

Morgan Varnado (OPRFHS class of 2019. Four-time LTAB member. College student—Brown University. Music producer.)

America Is Just a Negro in an Anthill

My southern grampa is as America a negro can be
surrounded by red ants. I don't know who owned his back
yard first, the ants or his lawn mower, but somehow
both found themselves in Mississippi
looking for food and a back to put it on.

My southern grampa is the absence of bugs.
His home is the places where we managed to scrape off
the cicada buzz like a hose scratching clean lines
into a muddy truck.
My southern grampa is most America when he's driving

up north to visit his grandkids. He runs
the whole Great Migration without taking a moment to rest.
My southern grampa sits in my living room, pledges
through the wet filter he calls country tongue
and I forget which end of the nation I'm sitting on.

America slips from my southern grampa's mouth
like the name of an old cousin long moved away,
a game he used to play in his youth,
a song he used to sing with the ticks
before they started biting.

My northern grampa is just a southern negro
who bears the winter to avoid the bugs.
One time, a spider had the gall to show its face
in my 1st-grade classroom. I reached out my arms
to protect it as we shuffled to the front door,

covering it from the spit of my classmates
who wanted it stomped.
I think I mean this when I ask my northern grampa
why he never played with Emmett Till.
Why he never was a blanket

to protect him from the cicadas, or the boot.
When my grampa replies, "He was just another kid
from the next neighborhood over,"
I realize no one knew Emmett could be squashed.
Both of my grampas tell the same stories

while scratching the same bug bites.
Ain't god make us niggas itchy.
My favorite game to play with the bugs
is "guess who's the one infesting my home."
The bugs always point the first finger,

spit out the first name,
bite toward my family.
To be America and a negro is to come from a long line

of homeless people with bug infestations.
There isn't a part of my family tree that isn't smacking its arms:
either squashing insects or confusing itself
for what's crawling.
America is as much a bug as both my grampas.

When it sprays pesticide, it coughs, too.
My southern grampa's home is infested.
My northern grampa's home is considered the infestation.
And I'm sitting here wondering whether to reach for the bug spray
or crawl to the nearest anthill.

Hannah Srajer (OPRFHS class of 2013. Two-time LTAB member. BA in history and poetry—Princeton University. Pursuing law degree and PhD—Yale University. Cofounder of nonprofit Tight Lipped. Political organizer.)

The Lamppost Glows Orange in the Daytime
after Larry Levis's "The Cry"

Then, everything rusted.
Little cream and pink houses,
rusted by nonstop sprinklers,
mice rusted to the dark
soil in their burrow holes.
The ants rusted to red brick.
On Lenox, the lamppost
glowed orange in the daytime.
My littlest brother sat in the room
facing the backyard, rusting out
answers to impossible math problems.
In my father's suit closet, the clean ties
rusted to old hooks. Mars, hidden
in the sky, rusted for the last
hundred thousand years.
In the red living room,
eggs deviled on an open plate.
My mother rusted to her black velvet dress,
her exposed ankles like two
hard, yellow-white teeth.
The women my father slept with
sang a song out of an open window,
the frame rusting in the wet morning.
We kept the notes dangling
on the front porch in long metal
tubes, a wind chime we hear
only when we are very
quiet, still in our mourning clothes.

Cailynn Stewart (OPRFHS class of 2011. Two-time LTAB member. BA in middle level education—Illinois State University. MA in educational administration—Concordia University Chicago. Mother of one.)

Birth

I. My mother's smile hard-presses across her face when she recalls my birth. Girl, you ripped me so bad that I needed stitches. The story of my survival. She enjoys explaining the irony in how those birthing complications made us close.

II. When I was born, I came busting out my mother's womb, stretching her like the gap of an overused bow and arrow. She bellowed as I came thundering through intestines, knuckling through her insides. I'd like to imagine that my father was there, anchored somewhere in the room, sweating. My life has continued to mimic this routine of being ripped and stitched together again.

III. It's senior year and I'm sneaking to my boyfriend's house. A long night with burned-out skies and shivering stars. We talk about how Chicago isn't built for Black, how our single mothers are the lightning and the bolts, how college is a bubbling blister at our ankles, how we make mantles of our skeletons and display them only to those who have felt the flames or the explosions.

IV. My mother, begging and leaving voice mails drenched in her cries. I know she doesn't mean to push me away or hold me too tight. I'm wondering how she's survived all these years. Was it her prayers that buzzed in her closets like bewildered bees? Or was it just me?

Ricky N. Brown (OPRFHS class of 2007. BA in Japanese language and literature—North Central College. MA in theatre arts—Eastern Michigan University. Former actor and English teacher in Japan. MFA in theatre—Sarah Lawrence College.)

Middle of October After Hours

I'm somewhere between
an anecdote about a musician and smiles
radiating heat off of a pair of brown eyes
stumbling down
back streets of a station
in suburban Tokyo snuggly secured
in the grip of a hooked
forearm, her tiny hands
locked with mine.
Suddenly, the neon blue walls and cold sky burn
with a searing flash of red light and an elicit siren.
I sweat.
She notices the steam hazing from my skin
dampening her cloth, 100-yen store gloves.
My eyes hollow and my spine stiffens.
We stop mid-stride, mid-conversation.
I forget all about the three hours we spent
bouncing around a dimly lit basement
to her friend's live band performance
or that hour train ride
where the world's most polite people seemed to climb over each other's
drunk and tired carcasses to fit into the last train's schedule,
forcing us forehead to chest between Shibuya and Saitama.
I could never explain to her how my voice, so mountainous,
spirit, so volcanic,
could shrink into an anthill
behind the emergency sirens.
I could never tell her about the night I spent as a 17-year-old

under scathing reds and blues and scorching searchlight
frosty heater to temple, knees in calves and spine,
the thuds of batons on flesh,
the eyes of willfully watching neighbors locked
on our young Black bodies,
squirming in the chaos as if it were some cast-iron skillet.
My sister and friend begging
for reprieve, for answers, for anyone watching to speak up.
That f*#king dog barking. It always barked by the gate.
The owner heard it and moved it
but he chose to stay and to watch,
maybe with a smile. Definitely without words.
The mistake without apologies or badge numbers.
Just enough freedom to get up and go without further
questioning . . . good enough for the Negro
way back when in 2006.
I couldn't tell her that EVERY TIME I hear sirens,
see flashing lights,
the sky turns to cast iron atop the highest heat
and I shift back to being a senior in high school,
hoping my motions are slow and obvious enough
not to be seen as an attempt to harm
so that I'd be free to go again without question.

Maggie Farren (OPRFHS class of 2018. One-time LTAB member. MA in English literature—Boston University.)

Palms.

i.
I miss the rev of the minivan.
The time I turned too sharp off Harlem and dug
its battered side into a white van.
The tobacco glued to the man's teeth as he yelled
and then realized that a minivan could do no harm
to his white van.
I miss pleading to my mother for the keys or slipping them
into my pocket, depending on the furrow of her brow.
And how I would drive the car until the red arrow just graced E
and then vacate for a week until the tank magically filled itself.

ii.
Driving at night is mostly like soaring,
like a pair of ice skates and the whole town,
your whole world, is frozen over. I'm always finding excuses
to run errands in the moon's embrace, to slip
down the driveway into brake lights and exhaust pipes.
I know neon Jewel Osco like I know my own knuckles.
The checkout lady, a cool breeze as she makes up
a family for me and wonders why they let me go out every night,
for dish soap, tampons, a thank you card,
wonders why shopping has become my good-night kiss.
Sometimes I will take Harlem Ave. so far
that cross streets become strangers and I wonder if I say
hello enough times the world won't feel so much
like a vengeful tongue.

iii.

I do not drive in Boston,
I take the train, the slow chug of the city's arteries.
I step onto Comm Ave. after a car passes,
jacket blown open wide.
I remember the thrill of a steering wheel
and a half an hour in which no one will call your name.
I daydream about Thanksgiving break
when I can shiver in the front seat,
puff clouds of smoke with the car as it awakes,
used to slumbering in its old age.
I will take the car down Harlem Ave.,
past Roosevelt Rd. where all the cross streets
turn to numbers and I will count on my fingers
the hours until I leave.

Kara Jackson (OPRFHS class of 2018. Three-time LTAB member. College student—Smith College. National Youth Poet Laureate. Musician with an album under September Records.)

portrait of venice with a side of pasta

we split a package of gum on the sun deck. it has never been this easy to get to the shore. if the city sinks, at least our purses are new and italian. we knew leather could tote a little water damage. i pretend the limone gelato is vegan. today, we don't mind a little diarrhea. after all, the bowels would be italian! we have been there long enough for our digested food to be american no longer. on the water, a tour guide talks about the boats but not who built them. i sneak out of the tour line to share a seat on the rocks with a dominican boy who is quiet, but knows who built them too. back on board, he and i have the audacity to share legroom. at home in america, my auntie is afraid of water. she cooks pasta in her own fear, runs a bath with her own history. my uncle, her husband, is dating a new woman who is too young to know why it isn't okay for me to like water this much. even in italy, where mosquito bites are itchy kisses, and a brown boy has never looked so good in the sun. in a worn-out castle, we make jokes about european efficiency, how a train can outrun anything it needs to forget. and my auntie is still stirring.

Leah Kindler (OPRFHS class of 2018. Three-time LTAB member. BFA in creative writing—Emerson College.)

Why I Write Poetry
after Major Jackson

Because I could say my friends' exes live in a swamp in my heart
        and no one would ask what it means.
Because my head is level and my wrists are narrow.
Because after block parties and cookouts my mom corralled us
        into the bathtub to wash dirt from our soles.
Because nowadays I go to bed with unwashed feet.
Because everyone who didn't eat breakfast in my house hates grapefruit.
Because instead of letting people in, I rebuild myself around them.
Because it haunts me that my aunt would still be alive
        if she had health insurance.
Because I still think about characters in books I read at age eleven
        now nameless and faceless.
Because all my poems end up in AP style.
Because I always have a crush on someone taller than me.
Because I can't find anyone in New England who knows what it's like
        to ride the Brown Line over the Chicago River in summertime.
Because my best friend and I have different words for love.
Because I'm still afraid to die.
Because I rode Razor scooters on the blacktop with the boys before school.
Because walking through Boston feels like spitting out cold air.
Because I spent a Valentine's Day at a funeral I couldn't cry at.
Because the winter always makes me like this.
Because I don't know what I mean by *like this*.

Camila Gamboa (OPRFHS class of 2021. College student—University of Illinois-Chicago.)

Plucking into the Next

Mexico is a baile on Friday night
A song that may last a few minutes
But have my Tias gleam in sweat
Discovering a new diet
They might actually maintain
Returning eight years later
Only to see that to them we never left
Time is unable to keep up with the cumbias that never end
For bringing someone onto the dance floor is not a question
But an invitation to live
To swirl with the night that isn't going to slow down
A fast-paced rhythm that makes the blisters worth it
To have the mariachi come
Play their paid-for songs
Then bond with all the husbands' wallets
Because the only thing ending is the night
Plucking into the next

Camara Brown (OPRFHS class of 2013. Two-time LTAB member. BA in urban studies—University of Pennsylvania. Pursuing PhD in American studies—Harvard University.)

Taking Down a Confederate Flag in Lincoln Park on June 27th, 2018

Alex offers to kneel, so I can stand
on her. A knee cannot hold me.

She asks if I feel comfortable sitting
on her shoulders. I showered this morning,

but my inner thighs are moist with trapped
heat from the sticky afternoon—crossed under

a billowing skirt on a sticky day.
But it has to come down,

so I climb on her shoulders as she squares.
She shakes as we rise. Her sister has her

hands in the under of her shoulders—just
in case. We are quite the tree. Families

walking on the grassy path or driving
to meet their friends glance & name us:

two late 20ish white Jewish women holding
up a mid 20ish Black woman: hands on

my sinking ass & shins. Again, I hear my mom
nagging from the magical corner of the kitchen

I could never find. She's whispering *put some elbow grease
in it* as I clean a cast-iron skillet with who-

knows-what leftovers. Up here, it smells
like barbecue, exhaust & some freshly

rolled grass. Even though I never drink beer,
I scrape with the metal can opener on my key

ring. I scrape & drag with grease & a prayer
I didn't make. Keys ringing like wind

chimes in a dishwasher. I scrape the flag off
the NO PARKING sign, start with a pattern.

I scrape in a thick X, stretching the stars jagged
& spill their white in the empty blue space.

Then, I peel off the red in each of the four
triangles until all that's left is a white 3 by 5

rectangle scratched white. No red, no blue
left. At some point, I start picking at the thread

of colorful traces. They look white, but I feel
them lifted like thin sticky scabs, an annoying price

tag. It's so quiet up there except for the dull
pluck of my nails against the now white sticker.

My wrists ache, but I don't stop till I hear
You think that's good? I say *obviously not.*

*Are you okay? Do you need anything? You seem
so calm.*   I say:

most days I feel like I'm holding
back a wave. Even now, there is so much

more I should say. Alex asks *How would it feel
to let it crash?* I don't know if the question

offers a safety pin or a boat. We walk
down the path where others passed us.

It is so humid my thighs say *thank you*
for the breeze & the water

builds up in me—some goddamn
metaphysical dilemma. No longer

embarrassed by my sweat & its bitter
breath.

As a student at OPRFHS in 1999, I was in Spoken Word Club after school when poet and MC Denizen Kane turned the corner into our classroom. Denizen, I'm telling you, can transform a classroom into a sanctuary. When he read poems, he'd clutch one hand to his heart as if pulling it forward to hold out to us. He'd have his other hand lifted like a prayer guiding his verse into the open air.

Amazed, I remember raising my hand after a poem and asking about the process of writing, "How do you know what to write about?" He thought for a moment. "Write the poems of necessity," he said. "Write the poems you have no choice but to write." In the middle of the next poem he performed, Kane belted, "Change ain't nothing but pain but the only thing I'm afraid of is staying the same." And there it was—the volta, the point at which the poem awakens us from previous thought and turns in a new direction.

I'm not really here to talk about poetic devices. (There is much more at stake right now.) Yet here we are, standing at the road's edge, staring a volta right in the face. That eager device, that lurking angle, is an Italian word meaning *turn*. I always thought it just creeped around the edges of old sonnets, but now we are at the precipice wondering what happens if we make any sudden movements. The volta challenges everything and everyone that came before it. It's a frightening device, a winding wilderness. It threatens what we know to be true. Just past the road's edge, around that turn, is something we've never seen before.

Denizen's lyrics rang in my ear the following year as I stood by watching my friends leave for college or rent apartments in parts of the city I had never been. I kept working as a waiter at Mancini's Pizza, the same job I'd worked since I was sixteen. I still slept in my parents' basement. I knew how to play it safe. It took all I had to force myself out onto the road's edge and turn the corner. Growing up demands we adapt, grow, or fade away into a rear-view horizon. We need to confront the volta of our immediate lives and turn, however daunting, around the bend toward the unknown.

All of the poems in this section take place on this turbulent road, attempting to make sense of the joys and traumas of change and becoming. All of these poems confront the volta head-on, and though we may not share the same experience, we may relate to questioning the world around us, feeling out of place, fearing the dangers of the world, loving complicated people, struggling with addiction, body image, prejudice, or loss, and then finding out what comes next.

Maybe you will be encouraged to step forward and turn the corner you know is in front of you. Maybe you will see yourself mirrored in these stanzas. If not, that's okay, too. But stick with us—you may be welcomed into someone else's journey, understand them better, and through poetry, rise to meet the road ahead.

—**Dan "Sully" Sullivan**

Riley Moloney (OPRFHS class of 2018. College student—Sarah Lawrence College.)

When Dinosaurs Roamed My World

The last long-term relationship I had was when dinosaurs roamed my world.
I removed Minnesota memories from my five-year-old brain.
I am the new kid who knows more about Star Wars than holding conversations.
I learn everyone's name in Ms. Engstrom's kindergarten class.
And I've decided that I need to find the person I like, like, like.
Her name is Magali, and she isn't from around here.
The world she came from is some far-off desert planet,
a bit like Mars,
known as Mexico.
She'd build up my confidence like Duplo.
Now I'm more okay with making what our teacher would call
"inappropriate choices."
I'm not as worried about getting to the dinosaur toys first.
But the jungle gym is full of predators, and if you talk different,
you're easy prey.
My friends swoop down from the monkey bars and scuttle out
from under the turtle.
They ask her questions,
the usual kind . . .
"What toys do you like?"
"How far can you swim?"
"Can you jump over a wall?"
The biggest thing kindergarten has taught me is how children can be just
as prejudiced as their fossilized parents.
I try to protect her but I'm not the big dinosaur I'm pretending to be.
I'm just a kid, so is she.
We're too young to learn how hateful the world can be.
But ICE disagrees with me and doesn't think she is worth keeping.
They taught us division early, and I am the remainder.

The only memory the class has is the way she talked.
The only memory I have of her is a gift she left for me,
her little dinosaur.

Jada Maeweather (OPRFHS class of 2021.)

Unwanted pill addiction

In first grade I learn what ADHD is
Uncontrollably dancing to a distorted tune
No, I can't stop tapping my foot
I should be learning to form a proper sentence
I can't be like other kids
Everyone is asleep during nap time
But I can't stop who-ing—
I'm a night owl
Staying up for my next dose
I become an eager pill taker
Pills take away my appetite
Pills leave a lump in my throat every morning
Thick saliva sticks to my esophagus
My teacher says, *Jada is an excellent student now*
Devouring every compliment the class gives me with these pills
I've gotten used to the smell of the doctor's office
My prescription stays the same
But the distorted tune I have been dancing to has become a screech
While the pills fade like background music

Paige Wright (OPRFHS class of 2019. College student—Northern Illinois University.)

Destruction

Daddy's hands soak through my cotton web curls.
His fingers curve inward to try to eliminate the smell of burning hair.
My scalp cries out chemicals as I hunch over the sink.
I want Mama, but she's home miles away.
Daddy attempts to soothe the ache by adding shampoo
But he makes it worse.
He doesn't understand how to be gentle
Always tugging me back when I get too far.
He doesn't understand forcing my hair to untangle causes more damage.
Graceless fingers snag the waves at my roots
Not knowing to start from the bottom like Mama.
My back raises, the counter imprinting my spine.
My gut drops and tears fill my ducts.
I keep the sorrow hidden, rinsing it down the drain away from his wild eyes.
His unspoken promise to protect me withers once my spirals straighten
And he leaves me lingering behind lost and broken down.
He's ignorant to his role in ruining everything he touches
Letting my skin scald, burn marks trace me
Scarring over into something tough enough to resist him.

Itohan Osaigbovo (OPRFHS class of 2003. Original Spoken Word Club member. BA in English literature—Howard University. MFA in creative writing—Columbia College. Artist. Organizer.)

Hairesy

Miss Lyons,
I thought you should know:
Hold in personal comments
about children
the way you hold it when there's no TA
& you've had to pee
for three periods.

Fourth grade
was the first time I called another woman,
black or otherwise,
something derogatory. Four-legged,
and unforgiving.

I'm the only one who heard the word I regretted.
But since then,
I've often wondered if you
remember what *you* said.
The jealous licorice curling off your lips.
The scornful shun of a struggle you had to know.
black girl hair.

Black girl hair with its never enough,
its complicity.
Its rejected complicated-ness.
You know the way it is.
Hair is never named beautiful
when you're Black girl.

Even if the ripe vines
protruding from my soiled scalp
were the hair version of your dreams,
you shouldn't have said it:
"People pay good money for that hair."

Words pawed my face in resentment.
Deep-fried my confidence.
Dubbed me least favorite
when sole black girl
was enuf.

You made it   obvious.

        At eleven,
I should have been allowed
            to express distaste
for the awkward
            I wasn't old enough to appreciate.

The space you reigned
            could've sang solace
when my strands didn't dance
like white girls in class
        or holler like afro pick heroes
        fisting the air in beauty
        supply windows.

I thought of my sandy spurs—wannabes
                        not fine, not thick.
    I wasn't proud of it.

Maybe my mane provoked my
elementary alienation,
        but you cemented it.

That day,
        I married "different."
And spent the ceremony cowering
beneath your unkindness
        licking the foul language
nestled between my whispering lips.

My vows, unoriginal,
and childish.

Adam M. Levin (OPRFHS class of 2007. Three-time LTAB member. BA in Latin American, Caribbean, and Iberian studies—First Wave program at the University of Wisconsin. MA in English education—Roosevelt University. Rapper. High school English teacher.)

I Gave You Power
A Golden Shovel after billy woods

Tony yanks a shotgun from under the tub, his knuckle kisses the lock on
    the **trigger**
and my head is a tropical storm of **warnings**.
The summer before, I asked my dad to find me an internship **in**
a recording studio. He told me, "No. I heard **every-**
one there packs guns." None of the studios where I'd recorded a **verse**
carried anything more dangerous than a mic stand, but **you-**
nger me followed my father's words like a trail of breadcrumbs you **can't**
find an exit with. But it was finally happening. I could **feel**
my arm bending under the trigger lock—my body knew **it**
wasn't meant to rack and unload a shell casing, knew **if**
I even considered loading **it,**
my hands would morph into maracas. Tony smirked and said, "Feels
    powerful, **doesn't**
it?" He didn't take the shotgun away from me until my skinny
    shoulders **hurt**.

Jesus Govea (OPRFHS class of 2019. One-time LTAB member. College student—Columbia College. Older brother of Abigail and Anabel Govea.)

The butcher taught me how to high school

In the car
my dad asked me
what I wanted
to be

And I just kept staring
at the motoring yellow marks
that skidded below me and wished
I could've rolled along with them

Because the answer I had scared me
Every dream that I've ever had
placed me in a waste bin
that housed the unwanted swole
and bulge of my figure

I ate all my body fat
but I'm not who I want to be
Cutting bathroom mirrors
with the turn of my jawline

I chiseled and chipped at myself
Thought the weight of my being
would size down with the ring of my gut

but when I learned
that mirrors lie more than eyes do
I sawed I amounted to nothing
Cuss out my reflection
because I knew

that the words that bounce
back hold no meaning

Cause the only thing I ever wanted
to occupy was my own skin
Although it seems that I will never be fit for the job

How do you lose 50
pounds and still feel
the same weight?
My confidence is still shot
And the shrapnel sits in
my face I hunger for more
of my old self

slurp every last flaw
Nothing goes to waste

Back in '15 being
fifteen not a fit teen
I bent the bleacher
beams watching football teams
and no one seemed to notice me
Tried to hang with those
in my classes but whenever I spoke
they reacted like my words were molasses
slow, dense, and compacted
Like their cheesecloth egos would
blacken if they sat with the fat kid

No one ever told me then that 200 pounds
would equal two straight years with no friends around
Five semesters with my head down
talking to the lunch tray
dancing by myself chopstick-stiff at homecoming

It's so numbing
to hate the flesh you bathe in
to feel hollow inside when all that matters is taken
out and carved leaving your soul with a jagged splint
When the only thing you ever wanted to occupy
was your own skin

A fork and spoon were my favorite couple
My bass was three times the average treble
Mentally I wasn't on this orbit
Flew to cheesecake moons in space shuttles
They say the fullest are the most fulfilled but this is rebuttal
'Cause what are love handles for
if there isn't no love to handle or cuddle

Juliana Sosa (OPRFHS class of 2021. One-time LTAB member. Gold Key Recipient—Scholastic Art & Writing Awards. College student—Knox College.)

You're at home, speak English, Mexican

You're at home, speak English, Mexican
But I have more than one home where I don't speak English, Mexican

My light skin doesn't show them I'm Mexican
Sosa tongue got them running in circles, Mexican

I won't be thrown over the border type, Mexican
But my daddy might, Mexican

I won't be chained in cages, Mexican
But my baby cousins might, Mexican

The 1st generation type, Mexican
I gotta make my dad's wet back dry with a diploma, Mexican

You go to a fancy public school, Mexican
The *I got white privilege*, Mexican

Does the Spanish that leaps from my tongue have privilege? Mexican
It doesn't write the air in cursive but spits dirt on my father's boots, Mexican

I translated my father's stereotype turned addiction, Mexican
Beer bottles wishing they stayed in Mexico, Mexican

We only go to Church on Christmas type Mexican
Beat our hands on our chest to scare the sin away, Mexican

I practically raised my baby cousins on my hip, Mexican
Do these hips scream Mexican?

Or do the stretch marks on them show how fast I had to grow, Mexican
To translate from teachers' offices to courthouses at the age of 6, Mexican

I got the *what to do if your Tía gets pulled over* talk, Mexican
To convince officers that green cards turned brown are still valid, Mexican

We come in different shades of pride and regret, Mexican
But I came to fulfill a dream that my father regrets, Mexican

Noelle Aiisa Berry (OPRFHS class of 2011. BA in musical theatre and film—Columbia College. Actor. Entrepreneur. Older sister of Nicholas Berry.)

On the Bottom of a Swamp

What I remember most about 5th grade,
besides the reds and pinks of dresses worn at recitals.
The ones Mrs. McDaniels cooed over, begging me
to smile more,

or the boy I kissed, tasting sweet for the first time
before I could even prepare for how green eyes made
me erupt blush. I recall the study of the layers
of rain forests, bottom to top.

Emergent trees that stretched, demanding to be hugged
close. The canopy bright birds could hammock beneath.
And the understory. I used to close my eyes onstage,
tilt my head down,

as if one could see their clear reflection in mud.
And though my loving audience probably sang
"I love you's," I could never hear it.
I'd always thought the understory to be like my smile.

It hides forest floor,
the way you hide grinding teeth,
the sun never truly kisses its bare skin.
I'm sure it tastes like the absence of sugar.

And though dark, its brightly colored critters warn you,
"Here lies swamps bottom." For all of the forest's
beauty, Mrs. McDaniels never warned me that rain-
forests and our minds match at every layer.

Any misstep could lead lips to Swamp's Bottom.
It tastes like throat's back, where bitter things hit you hardest,
shoot their best shots. She perhaps never saw that through my smile
I'd blush neon—"Warning! Kid afraid of her own voice!"

Most likely because I had volcano sound and mole hill
body. Whatever case, I never expected depression
to have a pretty colored warning sign.
Wouldn't be till 14 I'd have the courage to stretch

toward sunlight or at least reach for a pen, a mic.
Be challenged to open my eyes,
lift my head above canopy,
find that sun smiles back demanding to be kissed.

Grace Gunn (OPRFHS class of 2019. Coordinator of Black Affairs Council; college student—Southern Illinois University. Younger sister of Majesty Gunn.)

If I Made a Movie About a Preacher's Daughter

She wouldn't be caught in the church closet shaking shelves
or sitting in the front row with a cover cloth on her thighs
hiding the thick, stopping the too-short skirt
I'ma write a scene she can lay hands on "miss ma'am" that speaks on her hips
She'll let herself be mad in church,
tell the mother her jaws are too stiff to smile
She'd dessert "pastor's kids be the baddest ones" on every member's tongue
Pour a personal statement in the Sunday program
to tell them the bishop's wife has the same struggle
as the drug dealer's girlfriend
The first family's health is last in the announcements
Why does the congregation act like preacher's kids can't cry too?
Didn't Jesus weep on the cross?

Claire von Ebers (OPRFHS class of 2020. College student—University of Illinois.)

Auto Boy

Last week the boy in Auto Shop said, "Like, I'm not trying to be sexist, but you're the most technologically advanced woman I've ever seen."
And I bit canker sores on my tongue trying to spit out a "thanks."
What I should have said was,
"Every syllable in that sentence stabs my femininity."
And I want to tell him about the time
I was catcalled walking home from school,
how a middle-aged man slowed down his car just to get a whistle in,
and that my girl friends hold keys in their knuckles like
Wolverine when they walk alone.
The biggest fear I have is being a girl.
Auto Boy doesn't know I cut my hair hoping fear would fall with it,
that I cried when it didn't.
I wonder how oblivious he has to be to not realize that women are fighters.
I wonder what he would say to every girl
who fistfights their words to get an education,
or to women who've had their work shoplifted by loud business suits,
or every woman writer who had to use a man's name to get published.
Next time, he should probably chew his words more carefully.
And even in the end, he still had the audacity to utter,
"Like, uh, sorry, I guess."
I said it was okay, getting too entangled in his plastic-wrapped apology.

William Walden (OPRFHS class of 2001. Original Spoken Word Club member. BA—University of Illinois. JD—Northwestern University. Lawyer. Father of two.)

An Open Letter to Mozart

Amadeus,

This is strange.
Every time you appear,
I see my father,
huddled next to the lamp,
meringue and backlit,
hoisted by the couch.
The living room shedding itself
in layers of darkness and gold.

The walls behind him bare.
He sits next to his cabinet,
the silver and black
stereo, shelves, discs,
vinyl, and headsets jammed
onto shelves like honeycomb
filled with mercury pellets
and coal.

He listens to *An Chloe*.
Conducting it,
as a foreperson would,
waving cars around into the night.
What do you know about this,
Amadeus? This is strange.
You are dead,
and I am Black.

My father took trips
with his siblings
in the summers
as a child to North Carolina.
There were five of them,
relieving themselves
on the side of the road
to avoid truck stops.

You learn precision and shame,
pushing yourself out
into layers
of darkness and grass.
Pushing yourself out
while cars slip by,
humming into the night.

My father liked you
because of your precision, Amadeus.
Your phrases, coiled
and poised with design.
The same way he wanted me
to speak English. He would say,
"Learn to speak King's English."
"Speak proper English."

This was the same to him
as urinating in the grass
to avoid highway truck stops.
My father studied
bacterial and viral
pathogenesis,
and teaching me English
was his attempt at inoculation.

My father gestures
during *An Chloe*
as if it might bring about his revolt.
I am sitting across the room,
writing in English.
The first Molotov cocktail
between my father and I, formed.

Jalen Daniels (OPRFHS class of 2020. Rapper and skateboarder.)

Ethic

I was the kid who tried finessing school As and Bs
Doesn't work well in high school, cause now I'm making
Cs, or every letter you can have as a grade, transcripts
making it seem like I hate to stay, managed
If school years were the joke, freshman year was the butt of it
Didn't do any type of work in my math class,
Failed the semester, I knew I should've cuddled it
Cause every class taken deserves some study time
Should've took a break from nutty rhymes, got stuck in the silly putty
Next in nexus like Michael McGillicutty
I felt so debased, veins turned acidic
I didn't have the drive like I was low on fuel
and only took diesel like *The Chronicles of Riddick*
I question my past and if my future's still bright enough
My habits are like allergies, can't use your fist to fight the dust
I have to learn how to manage time
Start with my work so I can get to the outlandish rhymes
These problems need solving, only way I can succeed more
High school feels like years in isolation, I don't need 4

Tymmarah Anderson (OPRFHS class of 2015. Two-time LTAB member. BA in anthropology and informatics—University of Illinois. Research advisor—dscout software.)

Southside with You

    after Tyehimba Jess

1.
When your man comes home from
the trap, when he comes back shattered
and you are the glue—
when he comes back with heavy pock-
ets and fingernails down to the skin,
you got to rinse him down first.

Like the first time I saw his dirty money.
The smell gripped me harder than his charm did on our first
date—harder than his grab would on our last.
He was the rough edge Daddy warned me
about, but I saw his feathered insides.
I knew I could make him moral again.

2.
You got to have the backwood and dope
shaved and drowned, waiting for the day his
pores smell legal again, like before the streets
chewed out his body and spit him
soulless and without consequence into smoking sunshine.

I remember meeting the real him,
the day I gave my attention to someone else in his presence,
he became a kingpin,
a street legend who made his mark.
He called me a hoe—
gave me a bruised heart to match the one on my arm.

3.
You got to buff down the drug house blues
from potent skin, bathe away the gun pow-
der
from ankle and wrist, soak the blood of a traitor
free from his hair, scrub death and addiction
from the scarred and the gen-
tle, the love and the hate,

the dented and the indifferent.

The day I tried to leave him,
he couldn't decide which one of us was the real traitor.
A blend of "I love you" and "I hate you" flooded my
phone. He dealt with me the only way he knew how—
a game of Russian roulette with his life and mine.

4.
you got to laser his heart,
the affection he will never feel—take arms and hand
and hand and fingers and cleanse slow with human-
ity, and when he leaves out again the next morning,
you wait at the door with a bucket and
scrub to rinse him tender and
back moral again.

Marlena Wadley (OPRFHS class of 2015. Two-time LTAB member. College student—University of Illinois-Chicago.)

Alternate Names for Black Women
after Danez Smith

stolen womb.
america's stomping ground.
massa's wet dream.

martha stewart of plantations.
silent.
hymn hummer.

broom jumper.
cotton plucker.
floor duster.

loud snarlin and
fury growlin
like rabid canine.

white baby's lullaby.
black boy's alibi.
whatever name
our parents slapped
on birth certificates.

a shriek fossiled in gravel.
blood stained on fingertips.
prayer for breathing
babies.

howl when guns, jail, police,
america, pronounce them dead.
sunday church hat lady.

booty bustin, hip hoppin,
thick-thighed, syllable breakin,
lip-clappin girl
from around the way.

chanel wearin bitch with nose in the air,
ain't neva been to
the hood,
whose daddy toiled
her through college.

trend-birther.
creatures carved from the sun.
looting survivor.
sirens.

God's first born.

Anandita Vidyarthi (OPRFHS class of 2019. College student—University of Illinois-Chicago.)

Bi, Bi Brown Girl

There are three things we never talked about in my house:
my adoption, sex, and gay thoughts
We have more secrets than furniture
They lounge on the couch and sit with us for dinner
Mama taught me
Taboos are for brown women
who have trouble conceiving
and are faking being ashamed of that
India is no place to be born a girl
The only thing my parents told me about sex
was that I was not supposed to do it or
I may have to birth another baby girl on Indian soil
which is any ground my father has wafted his curry scent
As much as we love its aroma
it makes him dry cough and scrunch his nose
The spice and oil from the pot burn him first
I've sat at the kitchen counter to think
and overthink of all the ways I could break the news to him
Wonder if one more family secret will still hold the house up
Hope to clear the confusion out of the air
My dad talks "liberal-y" while cooking me dinner
and I want to burn the truth in front of him

Ibraheem Azam (OPRFHS class of 2020. College student—Columbia College. Rapper/music producer.)

Loops

They want a specific incident that doesn't reoccur
From a kid whose life is a J Dilla loop
Plus, my memory fails me more than my teachers do
I'm living one beat at a time, every line and rhyme

Basketball, video games, hip-hop:
Thought I was unique at first
I used to blast A$AP Rocky until the speakers hurt

Turns out there was millions like me
Now let me take a look down my life's street

Circa 6th grade, before the mixtapes and a big change
I'd like to take it back to way simpler ways
I spent my days at the YMCA and came home to play 2K
Followed by a Jay-Z soundtrack, Cole & Kanye the next day

I used to dream of the NBA, never dreamed of an MBA
I know a lotta kids around my age group could say the same

I used to sleep with a basketball
Before the knees hurt, growing pains, now I'm a fathom tall
The Osgood-Schlatters slaughtered all good athletic dreams
They weren't meant to be more than adolescent fantasies

I got home on Friday nights, my legs aching
Hopped on the PlayStation 4, my friends waiting

Then I became a couch-warmer instead of playing
It's easy to stay at home without motivation

Combine that with a tad of asthma
And interest in rap stanzas
It's safe to say I found a different type of dedication

Patrick Chrisp (OPRFHS class of 2014. Music producer. Fashion designer. Rapper.)

I could have been a lot of things

I could have been a lot of things.
Ms. Walsh-Farmer figured me best as wasted potential.
8th grade was bitter like Momma.
The fruit picked from hours of labor too distant from perfection
she'd thought her seed would bear early.
I was bitter.
Friends soared through graduation.
My feathers embraced gravity too hard.
Flight was for the creature that understood escape.
I only knew my roots.
I come from a bitter taste and heavy wings.
Daddy has left from the same door since he was my age.
Momma's habits are older than me.
They grew me as the first seed to slip past their tree's shadow.
Act like there was no divot to slow my roll.
What is up doesn't only come down.
Here it has to spill out too.
I was bitter.
Momma didn't understand that.
Momma tells me, "If you don't get your sh#t together you'll be packing it."
I tell myself she's bitter.
Momma tells me, "Get yo ass up for summer school."
Momma hopes I grow in the summer.
I'm bitter.
Not ripe enough for high school.
The halls smell too distant.
I can feel the length of 4 years in the walk to the 4th floor.
My kind of tree doesn't bloom here.
Langston tells me to try.

Puts a seed to my palm.
Our trees are like.
Asia exhales apple pie.
She asks me to make my own.
It doesn't hum as sweet.
But the flavor lost its glum.
My words don't waft the shade of the tree.
They glide away from bitter.

Langston Kerman (OPRFHS class of 2005. Two-time LTAB member. BA in English—University of Michigan. MFA in creative writing—Boston University. Former high school English teacher. Stand-up comedian. Comedy writer. Head writer—*PAUSE with Sam Jay* [HBO]. TV star [Comedy Central, HBO's *Insecure*, Amazon Prime's *The Boys*, ABC's *Bless This Mess*, and Peacock's *Bust Down*.])

Who Does This Feeling Belong To?

I am nearly positive there are no other
Langston Kermans on this smoking earth.
Certainly not in *this* neighborhood.

How frightening to think
there might be another
who appropriates the prescription for my abscess,

who claims my lost packages,
who watches anime and sucks
juice between his teeth, the same as me.

I am 32 years old
and I have never known anyone's
heart attacks in the morning shower.

No monoxide pumped into a closed garage.
No true loss.
Even my first dog lived to 17:

She died quietly on a metal table,
the family encircling her
like a fleshy halo.

Dearest "other" Langston,
how many eggs have you cracked
to find the yolk pecked with blood?

HOME

The word "stanza" means "room" in Italian, and that's how I like to think of my poems—as small, bounded places I can enter to work out a thought, or wallow, or pace, or bang on the stupid little drum of my heart. I find my way in, and then, if I'm lucky, I find my way out. There's a comfort in this, in being able to take the space to briefly burrow in language before rejoining the land of the living—even when the stuff I find waiting for me in the room is hard: trauma's remnants, the atrocities of the present, the terrifying shapes of what's to come. Learning to find my way back to the door, in these cases, is something of an exercise in hope. As much as poems have sheltered me through the most difficult parts of my life, they've also provided the equally important service of sheltering my demons from me. Poetry can't make the hard stuff disappear, but finding its rooms can help free up some space for the rest of you to breathe.

As a poet who often writes about shame, intimate violence, and intergenerational trauma, a question I get a lot is: how? There are a million ways to answer this question. Some poets use persona to approach topics at a safe distance. Some construct elaborate, extended metaphors, or use tools like rhythm and refrain to make the poem a piece of art they can hold, rather than a confession to relive. A few choose to narrow down the task by addressing someone directly; others ask questions, or imagine alternatives to the way things are.

One thing most (if not all) poets have in common, though, is that they all become writers in community with other writers. And this is the advice I give most often: Don't do it alone. Whether it's a classroom, a collective, an after-school club, a weekly poetry slam, or just one other friend, writing communities help us. For those of us who have been made—by white supremacy, heteropatriarchy, ableism, and so on—to believe we're monsters, they can be places that make us feel a little less monstrous. And most importantly, when that room becomes too vast, too dark to navigate, they can help us find our way back out.

In this section, you'll find thirteen poems that peek into the darker corners of home: poems exploring shame, troubled family relationships, the aftereffects of abuse and addiction, and the difficult questions lurking in one's lineage. Some of these rooms have monsters. All of them have doors.

—**Franny Choi**

Natalie Rose Richardson (OPRFHS class of 2013. Three-time LTAB member. BA in English language and literature, comparative race and ethnic studies—University of Chicago. MFA in creative writing and MA in English literature—Northwestern University. National Student Poet of the Midwest—Scholastic and the President's Committee on the Arts & Humanities.)

My Aunt's Angels

They knock on cupboards & ribs,
steal mothballs from the wardrobe's dim corners
& patch them into their wings.
They scream when the kettle boils.
Their feet & fingers are webbed like geese.
Some bake bran muffins in blue children's aprons.
The kitchen, powdered in bread flour, a cloud they glide through.
Others wrestle the wind through a screen door.
When the doorbell rings, they flap their arms & chirp
their mockingbird throats.
They work in shifts, all night shining shoes.
All morning they brush her hair.
Some are secretive & break the chimes, so she won't
know their comings & goings.
Others dissect the basement mice & pin
the decorative bodies, splayed like fans, to the walls.
Their laughter rakes like tires screeching through a stop.
She begs them to stop but they only start a game
of tar & feathers.
She opens the door to leave, but more trudge in
ferrying beer bottles & shoehorns, tiny mouse bones dangling
from their teeth.
Some plant violets in the garden then wash their feet
so the dirt won't track in. Or so the violets won't grow
inside. Some rock her to bed & call her *baby;*

others roll their doll eyes & bite her fingernails to shards as she sleeps.
She once woke to a fistful of blood & feathers, believing
it a tiny bird she'd crushed in sleep.
Tomorrow, she will take a pill & they will leave in a mournful parade:
When angels leave us, they look like lost children.
She will spend all day counting their shadows like stitches
& washing that dead bird from her fingers' webs.

Eliana Gerace (OPRFHS class of 2020. One-time LTAB member.)

It's not that I have a nicotine addiction

When I was little,
I would sit on my mother's lap in the smoking lounge—
a room in our house dedicated
to nicotine swirling through a window fan,
to coffee mugs with milk rings round the centers,
to doodles left behind on yellow notepads from boring phone calls.
Somehow the smoking lounge has remained constant
in all of the five houses we've lived in.

I would flail my arms
cradled in my mother's,
ignorant to the danger she held
between her first and middle fingers
until I touched it.
Band-Aid on top of Neosporin on top of blistering burn
became routine when I was younger.
Came with nicotine levels
without the pleasure of indulging.
It's not that I have a nicotine addiction.
I'm just addicted to the idea of the relief it would give me.
To the comforting scent
of stale smoke
and mint gum
that reminds me of family.

It's not that I have a nicotine addiction.
I've never smoked a cigarette.
Never circled my lips around its temptation.
Have only greeted it at family parties
where every adult's pack is labeled differently,
but always presents itself the same way:
You lean in for a hug and it tugs at your lungs.

Last week I hugged my mom.
I inhaled deeply, expecting that fragrance
I have grown so accustomed to.
I pulled back immediately
because she hadn't dragged a cigarette in three weeks
because she had been trying for twenty-four years.
Because now she only smells
of mint gum and perfume.

Alice Atkins (OPRFHS class of 2019. College student—Rhodes College.)

The Fire

My mom's brother died in a house fire
yet Momma doesn't seem to care
about the flames in our home,
about the whiplash of syllables,
about the gasoline my brother spits out
when his emotions get too heated.

I told Momma once
that my brother needs a shrink.
It's been months since
she said she would speak to him
yet the flames are still growing,
the fire department was never called,
and every time I try to stop, drop, and roll
my words just turn to ash.

I wish I didn't wander to wash away the words
that blister,
words that finish light and strike
windows black,
words that reuse yesterday like my home is steel.
It's not.

I had to fistfight the flames to realize
my burn marks can't heal
in a house that's still on fire.

Hannah Green (OPRFHS class of 2017. One-time LTAB member. BA in sociology—Northwestern University. Medical student—Feinberg School of Medicine.)

Its gravestone will read: Here they lie—all four of them, together.

My mother tells me cracks in the ceiling of my childhood
bedroom look like veins. I know she is a doctor because
she cherishes pieces of this house like our bodies. I know
I am meant to be a doctor, too, because I do the same.
She says good night, caravans to the cradles of her bedroom,
thinks nothing of it. Two hours later, I am swaddled
in the dark I called home for 14 years, wondering
whether this house is anything more than a body.

The kitchen is a groaning heart post-arrest, cavities bursting
with a mother and three daughters, overflowing dinner plates
like clotted blood. The muscle that wouldn't quit when the turkey
burnt, or the dog died, or the drunk dad trampled downstairs
before rehab. The stove kept churning out oxygen, gave
the house something to breathe, gave it something to latch onto
when all there was was space. We can't measure the pounce of
the kitchen with an EKG. Can't take it to the emergency room
when it stops pumping. The kitchen quiets as it empties,
its thumping nothing more than a flutter.

The den is my mother's lung. The kind of thing you trust
until nicotine dyes it gray and you aren't sure whether cancer
hides behind walls. It is the habitat for words unsaid.
My refuge after my first breakup. The couch a stretcher for
a relationship lost. I called that room home for three days until
it coughed me out just like it did my sisters. Breathed something
into us and then out. I didn't know girls could evaporate
so quickly.

I want to call our bedrooms the capillaries. The hallways, too cliché, and nothing ever happens in the in-between spaces, anyway. I know my sister has stopped reading when the light snailing through the crack of the bathroom door simmers. My mom keeps her lamp on every night. I know my family based on how they fall asleep. I wonder what the bedrooms know that I don't. The walls of the vessel, single layer of cells that carries a family with the blood pressure to pop.

I don't want to talk about the bathrooms. They aren't a part of this body. They're the disease. My parents greeted divorce with the wave of floor tile. All five of us hammered into a room that groaned something pathological. The bathroom infected us all. Me, loyal to shower curtain, the privacy it gives, the way blood scrapes off porcelain so clean. My sisters, angled over the rim of the toilet after stomach bugs, or bad nights, or big dinners. Mom spends so much time in the bathtub that I wonder if she'll emerge a wet prune. Keeps the door closed, finds refuge under the faucet.

The house is over a hundred. Past its expiration of human. But each time the four of us find our way in, the body screams. The kitchen compresses, the den exhales, the bedrooms simmer, the bathrooms are quiet. Each time we come home, living returns. I know life expires, too. I've seen my father's body come close to caving. So when the house caves, retches out the family, I'll hold its own funeral. Lay the foundation into dirt, soil cascading over the bones of the family nestled underneath.

Dawson Pickens (OPRFHS class of 2022. College student—
Embry-Riddle Aeronautical University.)

Ghost of the Ghost

I can't wait for the day where I find out who I wanna be,
and I can't wait for the night where I can finally see,
the real person who's never seen in my dreams.
That subconscious ghost haunting me to death
like I'm the one to murder it.
People keep gunnin me down
to the point where I don't feel the bullets anymore.
Just the sound of the shot piercing my ears over and over.

This gut deep nothingness whenever I get to thinking too hard
and my mind starts transforming into a maze controlling how to get out.
Have I become the ghost of the ghost
that haunts the nightmares of my nocturnal mind?
The social outcast inside his own family?
Yes they joke and laugh and I play along
only until I get to my borrowed room
in which I can stay till I'm 18.
I'm always alone nowadays. Only at the institution of education
2 miles from where I write are people who want to interact
with me on purpose. Or, they stay on the applications
of socialized media
and they get even more depressed
because they don't get enough likes.
When I sit on the labored cotton seat and stare into space,
I see every sibling in sight just looking down
into the black mirror and deafening white screen
where all else stops turning.

The dimension my consciousness escapes to
can no longer tell apart reality from its games.
The ghost that used to please me no longer lives.
For it was killed within itself,
by its own mind,
trying to escape the dimension set for its cell.
The new ghost has come to start a reign of terror on logic,
while rain pours down cinder blocks trapping the captive even more.

Anna Van Dyke (OPRFHS class of 2019. College student—Marquette University.)

Dead Shadow

I'm the beggar at the shadowman's front doorstep,
the smell of blood under my fingernails
Scratching at wooden framed skin
Acid dreams roll dice for a favor

I want to change that moment
when you could still hear the thumb twist crack of our feet
on the library room floor we slept on
As he slipped through until it was dark
split so I saw four of him at once
the fresh-tickled speared smoke
the smooth hands of abuse
the blood of plants
Made me live so hard I was dead

Anna baby,
he was the first one to hold you down in the face of fear
in a room without walls for the watching
expensively auctioned your malnourished body after he was finished
No amount of love could keep him from leaving you

It was the softest punch a man could give
so I went to the shadowman's front door
to give me back the shadow he never could

Majesty Gunn (OPRFHS class of 2018. Studying exercise science—
Southern Illinois University. Cancer rehabilitation trainer. Older sister of
Grace Gunn.)

My Cousin's High

My grandfather was a smoker.
It's what killed him. That same smoke could end my cousins too.
My grandma is resilient.
I'm hoping the residue from her hugs lands in my attitude.
I know people who hold heartbreak like hot rocks.
They let it match in their hands while wallowing in smoky rooms.
I think that's me.
I think I want attention.
Maybe I'm the constant in every relationship because
I can't break up with me.
Because I can't let go of who I am.
A doormat to anyone who wants to walk into me.
I welcome them in and leave the door open like an abyss.
They come and go as they like.
Maybe I'm the lesson they're being taught.
Maybe I'm the placeholder in the equation, just an x waiting to happen.
They always seem to be stronger when they leave me,
like shoe prints, them with me on their sole.
They just get what they need from the foyer of the put-together pieces of me,
just to leave me in pieces.
Maybe I should have crockered a little more.
Maybe I shouldn't have let them pass.
I've never smoked before.
I get high off an encounter.
Maybe I am the problem.
The one you're supposed to solve.
My cousins are all smokers.
Maybe that's the only way they feel anything.
I feel everything.

Donorica Harris (OPRFHS class of 2006. One-time LTAB member. BS and MS in information security and compliance—DePaul University. Risk and compliance coordinator. Personal trainer. Small business owner.)

Samson

Tee-Tee you only used water in my hair.
Sitting at your feet, your voice, vital nutrients
interlocking your wisdom into each strand,
my hair became naturally strong.

Strong enough to carry my weight when Uncle J's closed
fists wrapped around 9-year-old pigtails for spilling
Skittles on the carpet. Combing through tear-soaked hair,
you detangled my thoughts.
I told you he hated that you'd adopted me
your voice restored my confidence. Told me I was wise beyond my years.
You'd talk to him.

Fast forward 3 years to find you beneath Uncle J.
Your hair gripped by the soles of his shoes.
In your nutrient-filled voice, you whisper to me, "It will be okay."
It wasn't. I learned brittle hair can only take so much before it breaks.

Your daughter Tiffany only knows how to perm
hair too thick to hear her 19-year-old wisdom.
Water not strong enough to part through tough silence.
I don't talk anymore.

Tee-Tee you only taught me to speak strength
but if Tiffany could reach through my stressed coils
I'd want her to know that I broke
when I read my forged name under "I love you Uncle J," in his obituary.
Last we spoke, he said, he'd always hated me.
I'd want her to know that through silence it's always clear,
my birthday will always be the anniversary of her father's death.
I don't know how to speak on it.
Out of fear of being brittle, I'd only relax my hair for you.
We'll have to let it happen naturally.

I dreamt I stood over Uncle J's headstone.
I felt you free my hair in the wind.
18 years of shielded thoughts relaxed down my shoulders.
Staring at your grave beside him, I heard you,
"It will be okay. What's broken can be restored."
I'm naturally strong.

mo Santiago (OPRFHS class of 2015. College student—Columbia College. Teaching artist.)

you can't fall in love with someone every day

sometimes you need to look at someone
and say   *f@#k off*
sometimes you need to look at someone
and say   *not today*
sometimes my mom looked at my dad
and said   *i hate you*

and she was the only one brave enough
to say it out loud and i would say ask my father
why he was better at fighting with his fists and
get some answers but reason must've gone out
the door when he pushed us out and i doubt
he'd want to talk about either of us

you see if you tell my father you know me
he will tell you he does not like me, that
somewhere in the world air is being wasted
and when you take a look i will happen to be
there, just breathing   my father cannot
fall in love with me every day   or maybe

he was just too busy, maybe he got distracted
by his own loudness and all the yelling he did,
the way he would belittle us   and then argue
and argue until it was just him in the room and
the point bit back because not even it knew why
he was so upset

maybe my father forgot how to fall in love with me
every day   i could remind him but i am afraid
because when i look at him i see myself reflected
back into myself and that's scary to remember that i am
as much him as i am my mother and as i am myself and
i wonder if my father refuses to love me as he does himself

Vann Harris (OPRFHS class of 2016. Two-time LTAB member. College student—North Central College. Library assistant. Rapper.)

Mixed

When I dream about having a mixed
kid, I have nightmares about her father
raping me in a shed. White men are
the most savage. Built to take blood
from the anemic. I'm afraid of my

high-yellow child because she will think
I hate half of her. She will be fifty percent
conqueror and fifty percent captured slave
who is fifty percent claws and teeth. A middle

finger to bigots; a victory for bigots. Blue
Island made me dream about blond hair and
blue eyes, a white boy with politeness in his
teeth. Even mutual attraction to white men

feels predatory. The only one I ever talked to
had eyes that were catfish-fried-too-hard brown,
and when he tells me, "I've dated Black girls before,"
he was just trying to lure me into a lynch knot.

For my proverbial daughter's father, I am
a mantelpiece. A feast. A storehouse for his seed.
My baby will be the sun in a jar of fog.
Murky chitterling water. The corners of crust

on peach cobbler. Every time she likes a boy,
I will recall the quaking of my thighs. The sneering
of my ancestors. I hope she never asks how we fell
in love. Her father will suggest she bring me in

for show and tell. A foolish ape with sperm constellating
the fur of the lower jaw. Who am I to ask my child if
her father is Columbus enough to turn her hunter?
He taught her to aim a gun in my womb, so I wonder

if she'll be surprised when I'm not naked on the opposite
end of the scope. When I dream about having mixed kids,
I dream about murder too. About my baby's father building
a kingdom of blood, straight from my indentured arteries.

Levi Miller (OPRFHS class of 2018. Rapper. Freestyler. Actor.)

black walls in a white home

imagine replacing a married couple
with brick and eliminate
the walls of a home, take away
the boundary line,
turn a dollar into vows,
turn a cop into his cousin,
turn a dead relative into someone
he met for the first time at a family event

this couple sits at this home, and I imagine
interracial love, I imagine
if one side ever feared being
with their partner watching television

does murder mean something else
with the other side present?

does the other side
imagine a corpse in bed
does love invite the past
to the honeymoon?

which side will protest during the wedding?

who's wrong when you both dream

on each other's shoulders
who will
wake up
who will
wake

will
you still show up if your kind killed
the other.

will
you apologize on behalf, or remarry
to someone
who won't
protest.

Christopher Montel Byrd (OPRFHS class of 2012. AA—Austin State University. War veteran—US Army. Photographer. Small business owner. Motivational speaker. Entrepreneur. Social worker.)

Darkness has become my new commander

There is a strike on sunlight,
clothing myself with shadows, wrapping my face
with my imagination, becoming satisfied
with being undetectable.
My pupils adjust to the unpredictable
and my steps follow vibrations to calculate my distances.
Sunlight doesn't harm my physical but it exposes
who I don't want to be. I cover
the traditional tan walls in my "dying" room
in black paint to feel relatable.
Red rockets glare but glare in my direction while
shaping into the shadows of a bunker.
Sparks from homemade rockets will expose
the true intentions within your personality
while shadows create equality showing the same
no matter what. Darkened rooms only lighten
when sparks fly from rifles. A calm
night in the desert feels peaceful
until you see lights of mortars flying
over your gear. Light exposes the bad
and darkness shields its insecurities.
My skin becomes undetectable,
creating shadows on my ceiling that keep me
company while the stars hold me hostage.
The only light I give permission to enter
is the moon's.

Zaire Brooks (OPRFHS class of 2019. One-time LTAB member. Leader—
Living History program. Rapper.)

Spiderwebs

There's something about spiderwebs that makes us twins in a way
To us they are an easy sweep of a broom to fix
In another existence spiderwebs are vast, made of a steel adhesive,
and impossible to escape from

I am a spiderweb
in a May conversation at the picnic table full of web swatters
My aunties and older cousins all have their brooms
lined up, ready to swing at me the second I'm spotted

You ever notice how spiderwebs just appear
in the corner of your basement and are only
problematic the second after you see them?
But if you never saw it, you go about your day
and reach for the top shelf unbothered
You don't question it or the creature of its origin
You wouldn't question the existence of the web
It would just be
like me in the '08 reunion—I never wanted to cause anyone trouble
so why are they trying to dish me into the dustpan on sight?

This corner's threads were tailored to my liking
until I ended up in the pile of younger kids the seniors saw as mere cobwebs
And I've seen people reach right past me a thousand times
to the top shelf with no problem
Guess I'll find a better corner or people without brooms

and ODES

On April 3, 2020, my uncle passed away at the age of eighty-five, presumably of COVID-19. Uncle Al had been diagnosed with Alzheimer's when he was in his early seventies. Funny, gregarious, wise, generous, and a tremendous orator, he was an instrumental figure in my life growing up. After his Alzheimer's diagnosis, I started writing poems about him to help me process the loss I was experiencing. With each visit and each phone call, his mind and memory were deteriorating in front of our eyes. The poems I wrote were a conduit, an ode to who he was and a way of accepting who he was becoming. After he passed, I sent a poem to my aunt and cousins as a form of condolences.

For my students and alumni, poetry has been a way of introducing their own children into the world, to celebrating the people they love, and grieving those they've lost. Loss can make us heavy and love can lift us up. Poetry can help us lighten the load and revel as we float.

After a loved one passes, we often think about the past. Shortly after Uncle Al passed away, my parents and I reminisced about the first OPRFHS Spoken Word Showcase: my coeditor Dan's stage debut. My parents drove to Chicago from Ohio to be there—we knew it was going to be historic, even though it was seemingly just a bunch of unknown teens reading their poetry. We still remember the electricity in the air as each student got in front of the mic in a packed theater. The hollers and snaps and claps from the audience, mouths agape at what they were seeing and hearing. That was an autumn night all the way back in 1999, and each of the showcases since then celebrates that moment and welcomes a new set of poets to be heard.

Two poets who participated in the largest number of those showcases became best friends in 2004 because of Spoken Word Club: Tabitha Hurdle and Nova Venerable, both of whom have poems in this section. Tabitha writes of missing her mother who passed away of cancer just a year after Tabitha's wedding. Nova writes about a completely different experience—the first days as a mother. Remembering, celebrating. Celebrating, remembering. In late May of 2020, I had a catch-up Zoom call with Tabitha and Nova—each of us miles and miles away from Chicago, but bonded by Nova's twelve showcases and Tabitha's eleven. On the call, we mourned the death of Nova's dog and celebrated Tabitha's new job at Twitter. I'm not their father, but they call me "Pop." I'm not their father, but I call them my daughters.

My uncle never made it to a showcase, but he is Nova and Tabitha's great uncle, even though he's not. That's the magic of poetry—it can make family of those who've never met. Poetry is smiling there with us at the beginning and helping us shed tears at the end.

—**Peter Kahn**

Grace Fondow (OPRFHS class of 2009. One-time LTAB member. BA in Spanish language and literature—University of Wisconsin. MFA in creative writing—California College of the Arts. Sales account executive. Mother of one.)

Lessons

A Golden Shovel after Lucille Clifton

After twenty-two hours in labor with minimal dilation, my **mother**
suggested we rethink the natural birth plan. She worried **I**
would be too tired to push when it came time. **Have**
you ever been ashamed by the magnitude of your own relief? I **managed**
to look at her face for the first time in half a day, saw the terror spread
    from jaw **to**
forehead like tide reaching dry sand. As my birth partner, she had to
    unlearn
her instincts, trade in her tender. I remember her pleading palms on the
    small of **my**
back: push-pray-push. She, a single mother, and now me the same. There
    are some **lessons**
we don't mean to teach. I have tried with my daughter's father. But **I**
refuse to raise a girl who tiptoes around volatile men, and I **am**
too tired to teach a man how to do good. My mom has said that when my
    dad **left**,
all she felt was relief. Sometimes I feel as if we are **in**
a loop. Our experiences coincide, collide, and swallow. This **otherness**,
this unspoken truth—may Phoenix unwind it, write it new when she
    becomes **mother**.

Coe Chambliss (OPRFHS class of 2007. College student—Los Angeles City College. Veteran—US Army. Filmmaker.)

Dad, I forgive you, 2013

In Kingston airport I'm leaving
my luggage at this gate.
This is where I bury
16 years of digging.
My arms have been busy
since our hugs broke.

I didn't know Spanish Town
or 'Buff Brentwood,'
owner of the broad-shouldered
house I slept in. A man that stood
mountainous. Against the sky. At 5'6"
built like an adoption agency.

His sweetheart was my sweetheart
Tasha
'cept he changed her diapers.

Fathered 5 kids
and ringed a wife
before immigration
broke their hug up.

5 kids he planted.
5 noses he sucked colds from
cuz "me no trust tissue on the skin of my yute."

"Is that you, Dad?" I'd think,
ready to drop my shovel.
The answer was no
and yes.

Imagine my "damn"
when bank account
shut down
the day after I landed
and Buff reached into
empty pockets
and pulled
routes to rooftops
for lunch.

Or the dance hall
intros kicked out of
his mouth
"me daughter"
and not "me daughter's friend"
even though I wasn't
and was.

Dad, I've been digging for you
since Chicago '95.
I'm still not at the bottom
of your turned back.
I dig
throwing fossil smiles
over my shoulder.
The deeper I go
I dig
like you're buried alive

in your mistakes
and need me to save you
before life sucks the snot
out of you.
I dig,
I cut,
I jab through the earth.
Screaming inaudibles into
years of space
until

Buff hugged the shovel
out of my 6-year-old hands.
It was a hug that was sorry
for your shortcomings.
And left room at the table
if I was ever back in Jamaica.
It was a hug
that even left room
for you.

Jamaal James (OPRFHS class of 2004. BA in marketing and MBA—DePaul University. Radio DJ. Two-time Daytime Emmy winner for original music. Founder of music licensing company. Product manager for residential and commercial lending.)

Return to Sender

Hold her frigid hand,
sit at her bedside.
Days earlier the call came.
She was in the hospital,
words delivered like unwanted packages left at the wrong address.
Hospice prepares.
She spends her last days at home.
She is carried back to bed,
body limp with a weight too heavy to lift her suffering.
Instant thoughts of things I should have done differently.
I recall past conversations.
"As long as you did your best with the knowledge you had,
you can always take your learnings and do better next time."
I realize there'll be no next time.
Time.
Time can't erase regret,
only memories.
"I'm ready to go home,"
I remind her I finally brought her home.
"No, I'm ready to go 'home,'" she repeats as she gazes
around a house that no longer feels familiar to her.
Her words marked return to sender.
They could not be accepted.
Pleas that I'll be lost without her guidance
did not bear enough postage to be delivered to their destination,
lost in transit to mind at peace; unable to change.
She reminds me,

"A road does not end just because there's no more pavement to walk on,
create a new path and it shall be your own."
Deep breaths wilt into silence.
Every exhale revives a past conversation.
Wisdom carefully placed in envelopes,
stuffed into an overflowing mailbox
that's brimming with letters I thought had wrong addresses
waiting to be opened.

Iman Shumpert (OPRFHS class of 2008. NBA basketball champion. Winner of *Dancing with the Stars*. Rapper. Reality TV star. Clothing designer. Married to Teyana Taylor. Father of two.)

Pain

Auntie I'm sorry
if I ever felt sorry for myself.
You lived with something wrong
and ain't complain about ya health.
But losing you it hurt me . . .
and at the time I was on a crutch
so trouble hopped a bird
became a wizard with a dutch.

It was heavy on my mind.
I started missing the Chi
vs the Celtics you had us sitting courtside
and I love ya for it.
And now my life crazy
traveling with sh#t to do
and every time I see a flight attendant
Ima think of you.

If you was still here we could have a beer
a cheers lil rosé in the OJ for New Year's.
Don't worry 'bout Vince I got him.
We go back to training wheels on the bike when we started riding.

Can you believe ya nephew in the league auntie?
And everywhere I go got brand-new kicks on me.
You always said to be a man with at least a dollar
and when I get rich to always wear my blue collar.

So I go harder than that 9-to-5 guy that got his degree.
But he no smarter than me.
I be clean cut cuz Ahrii my barber.

I get the full course and gotta save on the starters.
I just wanna come over for Twizzlers and cream sodas.
My signature tight cuz you made me write it over and over.

Always hated you smoking . . .
so now when Erik grab a square I tell him leave the room
cuz that's gon make me think of you.

Seeing you battle cancer was a nightmare.
I don't know how my pops would spend nights there.
I know you was tryna fight but it don't fight fair.
I went and got us outta there.
I sweared wit my right hand to a stack a bibles
at Agatha with all the disciples right there.
And everyone else there to witness my bold statement.

You taught me self-motivation.
Wit no procrastinating or over-exaggerating . . .
and that's why I think I made it . . . so RIP AUNTIE.

Sierra Kidd (OPRFHS class of 2006. AA—Triton College. Senior certified pharmacy technician at Walgreens. Mother of two.)

Motherhood; Full Circle

She told me not to put coins in my mouth:
"Money comes from dead people's asses,"
she said. "Dollar bills too, Mama?"
Bathroom air smothered in Exclamation perfume
She rushed magical green lipstick on
with the closed end of a bobby pin
Magical because it turned red on lips
She melted the tip of her eyeliner
I watched as she swiped it across her bottom eyelids
like an active sketch on a drawing pad
with a smooth school pencil
She had scars on her face so old
they looked like birthmarks
and a chipped front tooth
Mother in her 20s with a chipped front tooth

All from beat-ups
Beat-ups by pimps, her baby daddies,
her sisters, somebody, and always
Beat-ups were regular for her back then
I'm still trying to figure out who is to blame
Because her troubles were always someone else's
fault Just ask her if she'll let you
Not us, her kids
Her daughters, and recently plural, sons

Dressed in her going-out clothes
Hooker clothes
"Where ya goin' Mama?"
That "I'll be back!" hit harder when
I knew she wasn't coming right back
"When Mama? Am I gon' need ta take care of Nip again?"
Somehow, she managed, "I'll be back soon, dammit,"
out of one corner of her mouth
with a lit cigarette hanging out of the other

All night I waited
All the next day too
Wasn't enough cars in all of Chicago
that went by the window
None of them brought her back
Like days, they kept passing
Nip and I ate suga' sammiches
Ketchup sammiches the next night
We took the biggest bites out of potatoes,
made a game of it to see who could eat the most
We chose nasty over hungry
I don't know what we did between those nights,
but sometimes we ate grocery ads

Almost like a dream come true
Our imaginations at their best
Closest we came to real, good food
That was Teressia, Mother,
Mama, Mom, Ma, doesn't matter
All of them left her kids hungry,
lonely,   just out here.

Christian Harris (OPRFHS class of 2009. One-time LTAB member. BS in business management with a focus on entrepreneurship—Bradley University. Small business owner. Community activist. Nonprofit leader.)

She Asked Me

Exes are like scars
Even once they heal
you still remember
where they were

She laughed and for the first time
all afternoon her smile did all the talking
I don't know what I was thinking
We would have never made this work
Forever is a long time—
Do you remember when we met?
Late night at the after set
Relocate the back room
Lights all around us
Place smelling like musk
I swore we were on the cusp
of something great that night
But you changed my mind
I let you
slip away
Look how things change.
Mama's even doing better she may
make it 'til next month or
maybe next year. Doctors aren't real clear
My family still asks about you
I think they hope a little
When you think about me do you get lost in time?
Could we have been fine?

Could we have made the long climb
toward eternity?
Eternally I'm conflicted
Internally I'm—
She stopped
"Regrets are worthless"
I said, "No, they're priceless"
You were priceless
We were priceless
Everything we did together
was worth something
Even the regrets

Camille Rogers (OPRFHS class of 2018. College student; major in Arabic studies—George Washington University.)

Green Chevy

Green Chevy, you bastard. Rolling wheels off-kilter, rest of the body moving faster than you could. It's time to drive to the cemetery. Grandpa plants trees there, Chevy. For all the soil-ridden bodies below. He plants trees there, Chevy. He's been serving his whole life. I'll sit on Grandpa's lap and hold your wheel, too big for me even now. He plants trees there, Chevy. So we'll put a hose in the back, and the dogs will come with us. Please don't chug-chug and break down, you bastard. Your thunks make me nervous. Grandpa doesn't listen to your radio. That kicked out a while ago. Blooming dirt from the road upped by your wheels. "Just look up," he says, and I do. We have to pull the hose out of the back. Why won't your back panel open, Chevy? Have to water the trees. You must have laughed, Chevy. A man and his 10-year-old granddaughter, watering trees for no one. This cemetery needs magnification. "Take care of things even when it seems mundane," he says. When you're mine, Green Chevy, I'll take care of you.

Tabitha Hurdle (OPRFHS class of 2008. Two-time LTAB member. BA in political science, BS in journalism, and MBA—Boston University. Engineering & tech recruiting coordination manager—Stripe, Inc.)

The Last Good Day

Mommy,
you love that your birthday is two days before Jesus's.
Decorations and twinkling lights
strung across snow-powdered windows and veined bushes.
The whole family wrapping up secrets, the drama
stowed away for your winter wonderland party.
This is the warmest night in a while.
Looking back, the photos don't quite capture
the giggling
of plush pajamas and fuzzy socks throughout our house.
The lightness and ease of laughter.
We both know
pictures are too still for that.

Your grandbabies hoard gingerbread between their gums
and cheeks,
powder sugar seeping through their pores,
pitter-patter leaving sweet trails along the hallway.
This year, your birthday wishes aren't stacked high
like snowflake cookies on our dining table.
I grab your fingers beneath it, secretly,
knowing these moments are the only gifts you asked for.

We should do this again next year, right Mommy?
We tried to tell them.
Soon, the light candled on red velvet cupcakes
will pause time just long enough to fool us all.

Singing will fill up spaces you'll evaporate from.
Then, you'll blow out candles and the dark will settle
like eyelids.
This day will have a photo-like still to it forever.

I'm still waiting for the morphine to numb.
A syringe to help me hoard our sugared moments between drying cheeks.
Just something to block the pain from seeping into my gums.
I realize how useless the body becomes
when it no longer fights with you.
A body that has birthed and fed. A body blistered and thinned.
A shriveled tongue salivates for pills the throat refuses to swallow.
Limbs are veined bushes too frail to hold lights.
The frozen shocks, relapsing, how *soon* freckled
so quickly like tumors colonizing your breasts.

This is how *is* becomes *was*.
The side of Jesus we don't celebrate on His birthday.
Candled cupcakes make us so easily forget when
He chooses not to heal and allow
modern day crucifixion,
when there aren't enough white blood cells
to count as stacked birthday wishes.

Merrick Moore-Fields (OPRFHS class of 2011. BA in animation, interactive technology, video graphics, and special effects—Hampshire College. Graphic designer. Animator.)

Bird

I remember Charlie Parker.
Ken Burns broadcasting bebop blues on
the flat-screen. My Dad's ears were glued to
the speakers
Cherokee was playing
a single song with subtle somber notes.
Dad heard a genius: mastering of craft created by the old band
unparalleled in the art of freestyle
but I heard different: a kindred spirit,
a sad bird crooning his pain and expressing grief,
singing sorrow songs, playing that depressive note
that coats notes with melancholy measure.

I remember my brother telling me, "Play on sax man!"
before death kissed him on the cheek in a crashing car.
Last words to me were go the distance,
"Play like your life was your last
show. Go to heaven with a shelf full of
awards. With that 1,2,3, and 4.
Goddamn son play those chords.
Lay off the brew: don't pour, don't smoke, play the track unaltered.
Don't falter: devil's asking you for a dance and a chance to make
bank.
Twist your brain like a Rubik's Cube
so your attitude ain't all depression and anxiety . . ."
They trying me, Jordan. Help me play the blues.
So they understand my pain.

Now, let's rewind: Mr. Parker, lost his best friend in a car crash.
That drive was treacherous, but told him to play on.
That song of sorrow sought solace in somber
notes.
I know that song all too well.
Everybody else told him to play on . . .
Medicate his pain with brew and dope,
hope to get on that tree branch so he could sing.
A bird with wings wanted to fly
but tied to the cage of music that was his own illness.
You played on bird, bit through the ropes so we could soar.

Peera Serumaga (OPRFHS class of 2022. Two-time LTAB member. College student—University of California San Diego.)

Transforming As My Mother

I sit with grandpa at his doctor's appointment.
He holds my hand with his words.

We wish for time to slow down.
An impatient phone call leads us back
to Rush Hospital. We grapple with our last bit
of hope and trace our path across the city.
There, I collect dust from stale air and beeping
monitors that have become all too familiar.
I walk into the room and
lift my mother's swollen hand.
This has the same effect as watching a clock

as time goes on. The pages left of her story grow thinner.
So I sit with a chaplain, my prayers stacking
into their own anthology
because God said there's power in numbers
but I feel alone in fighting and I'm ready
to be released from an endless loop
of hospital visits and imprisoning home life.

On Sunday, I reach into my back pocket,
pull out my last prayer to send.
The prognosis rolls past.
From there, it became clear words
have always been my savior. I lawyered
on her behalf though time continues
and her state remains unchanged.
Each of her breaths violent and oscillated but forgiving

and her ceaseless fighting proves
that you can be the author of your own novel.

Still, I touch the skin on my cheek
and feel numb, days of adrenaline
run my restless nights and every thought
of my childhood is a buried prologue.
My mind ticks to only the painful
memories because I've done just
as much transforming as my mother.

Today, my lungs take new breaths,
enjoy the air and time she almost lost.

Micah Daniels (OPRFHS class of 2020. Two-time LTAB member. College student—University of Illinois-Chicago.)

What Priscilla Was Like
after Patricia Smith

My dad told me he wanted to name me after Priscilla,
the Black woman who mothered my granny.
Books probably fit her fingers
the same way regret sat comfortably on my father's tongue

She had artificial curls long as a
pinky and a home in Tennessee
Lived her life scared of white people with pink
skin that threatened to make brown skin turn red
skin. She begged my granny
who then was just Barbara,
to be careful on Saturday nights, to pull down her dress
so the boys down the street didn't get any ideas

Priscilla wore slippers
made rough from too many cracked sidewalks
and threadbare rugs
She was never afraid to bend the slippers into a weapon
One that had my granny look past her last life
trying to wriggle out the best mistakes
that warranted a slipper beating,
the taste of concrete and fraying cloth

Priscilla's voice boomed out intimidation
and it made up for fragile bones
she passed on to Granny
and showed up opposite in the new Priscilla,

correctly named Micah,
with a salted difference of time zones
and a mother too light to bring me Priscilla's depth

Sometimes I imagine Priscilla is like me:
determined but afraid
Pessimism, a feature in her mind
Her teeth would come in crooked and backward,
branding self-conscious into her spine
and trying every day not to slouch
She would be afraid of the steps she would take until death

and wished heaven was like Neverland
She would be in love with a boy that will never love her back
because he reminded her of a time she was happy
She would have no rhythm and would love dancing anyway
Would talk in cursive lowercase sarcasm
and be asked repeatedly to slow down, speak up, and be nice

I wonder if my father loved Priscilla for these reasons
or if he loved her in spite of them
I hope he loves me more
I dream of Priscilla every
night and each time she's different
But always more beautiful

Novana Venerable (OPRFHS class of 2008. Three-time LTAB member. Star of the documentary *Louder Than a Bomb*. BA in psychology and BA in Spanish—Smith College. Premed—Columbia University and Loyola University-Chicago. Master's in clinical mental health counseling—Rowan University. Mother of one.)

Flesh of Mine

I.
My body is a ship strung
between the blades of a propeller.
It's 4:10 a.m.
I contract life until the curve of my stomach
is welded into a world where Black men
are born with bullets in their backs.
It took us 26 minutes to leave me a pulped wreck.

6 pounds 7 ounces and you don't cry.
I look for you,
watch you uncrease like the bends in my knees.
You yell at the doctor, a short growl
and I know that you are just like me
with a tongue too sharp to fragment words.

Your brown eyes droning the room.
My skin still hot from labor, pushing
heat into your pores,
our heartbeats drilled together by our breath.
You are as still as kisses I type onto your forehead
and I know that this is the only love
that will ever matter to me again.

Son, I'm sorry for being selfish.

For squeezing you into a life that I don't recognize.
But I need you to know that ya mama
ain't never been weak.

II.
I am an armada.

Endless sails snipped from horizon,
swimming sky to sea,
buried beneath blue burdens bouldered on my bows.

I bellow blindly.

Never needed a man
except to conceive.
A woman too loyal to notice the holes in my stern.

I soulmated the plank.

My masts married to holding the world up for everyone else,
iron rusting from my hair follicles, leaving behind corroded
pieces of the *me* we used to love.

I lost sensation.

But mommy's woke now.
And it didn't take the deaths of 300 men to align my fleet
or to force me to grow gills.

Just your love to unbind anchors from my tear ducts
and a wake-up call: Poseidon's Batman symbol,
Calypso's Davy Jones to keep my tunnel vision straight.

III.

Stink J.,

I will sewage nations for you,

seaweed the souls of every man, woman, and child if I have to.

I will never let your horizon cut itself like mine did.

Won't stand by and watch you sand into the ocean

until you don't know yourself.

Will never leave you without a battleship or protection.

Can't let your back oxidize under the pressure of being Black in America.

Mommy will grow your gills for you

so you will never have to feel your lungs backfire

cannons into your chest.

Jamael "Isaiah Mākar" Clark (OPRFHS class of 2009. BA in communication—University of Illinois-Chicago. Founder of Impact Mākars.)

Interstellar Birth

Doctors' stethoscopes were flying saucers,
rotating 'round his chest like orbiting planets.
Family and I shuttle into a waiting room
full as the moon on the night of his birth.
Claustrophobia made me feel like an astronaut.
I needed space.

April 11th, 2002 . . .
A star cradles a glow too luminous for 9 months
of hibernation in maternal galaxy.
Water breaks Orion's Belt 4 months
before it wraps around mother's waist.
He takes his first breath.
Lungs the size of birthday balloons before
breathing celebration into them.

Weeks later, Jayson arrives home.
His body the size of an average human hand,
holding 22 ounces of cosmic dust.
Light enough for gravity to question its own laws.
But he grew gracefully into a heavy heart.
Heavy like hearing him say "I love you" at the end of every phone conversation.
Heavy like watching him share every piece of his Milky Way with friends
just so they can taste how heavy-hearted this galaxy should be . . .
but it isn't.

Jayson wears hearing aids to keep up with the speed of sound.
His speed of thought travels on low fumes.
The medicine launched inside of his incubator saved his life,
but sacrificed his brain and some friendships.
Kids treat Jayson like he's from another planet.

But just because it takes some of us a little bit longer to develop into a star,

does not mean there is something wrong.
I think we keep forgetting.
Being born premature is just the universe's way of saying,
"9 months is too long. We need you here now."

David Gilmer (OPRFHS class of 2006. Three-time LTAB member. BA in creative writing—Knox College. MA in English education—Concordia University-Chicago. Father of two.)

In the ten seconds after you see that your wife is pregnant, but before you speak

When you see the two faint pink lines you will not believe—it is supposed to be harder—it cannot really be true. You will wait and wait and wait for some flutter—some warm dew breath—some soft firm grip to yank you back—even then you may not believe it. There must be some trapdoor somewhere. Some untethered fall. A pulling out of the rug—and you will tumble—all whetted elbows and blunted knees—scrapes and bruises—back to yesterday.

She will touch your hand and then kiss you—this is a new kiss—not the too much lip gloss—Dentyne Ice—firm and sneaky—long and wet—sixteen and sneaking in each globbered peck before home. Not the angry and rushed outside a bar—too fast and too hard—the wishing it could be longer but you've broken up months ago so you really shouldn't be doing this anyway, kiss. Not the beer and pizza kiss—the peckish smacks against the cheek in your first apartment. No—this is a new kiss. This is the *You're gonna be a dad kiss*. This is the—*I will still kiss you when the dishes aren't done and the dog licked your face after eating a crap-filled diaper and there's dried milk in my hair and our kid is sick and suddenly I am counting the whiskers on death's face and maybe there is not enough time so let's just grab on and stop everything because all I want is more*—this is the—*There's a lot to say so let's just skip it for now and kiss,* kiss.

There it is, two pink lines—and the sun splitting the room open on a cold Sunday. Day-old takeout on the couch in sweats crying at children in movies on Netflix. Warm socks—arms wrapped around a softly cresting belly—unable to tell anyone but so desperately wanting to blurt out—*Guess what my wife is doing?*

And then, when you hold him you will pray deeply. You will place each toe and finger on your tongue and you will speak to God. You will lay your rough cheek on the smooth of his bloated belly and swallow each wail—you will think of dipping him in and out of oceans. You will wrap him in a swaddle and practice bobbing in the surf—salt sting—his eyes smiling as he licks his lips—his long brown curls blonding in August sun. You will tickle his toes and think of cement—barefoot walks around the block—popsicle stick on chin—jarred lightning—smelling a lake storm blowing—green sky foaming like a creek. You will smell his crisp snow breath and cherish the clean silence of post-blizzard—red cheek sledding—the squeal of joyful falling—the piercing sound of growing up.

You will imagine an entire world—then give it up—because he will be born with one leg too short—or one heart valve not closed—he will be afraid of heights or allergic to air. The doctor will tell you steady and giant that he needs to stay overnight for observations. Suddenly Sundays are spent on trains going to and from MRIs—CAT scans—tests you don't understand—everything will be inconclusive.

At school his gym teacher tells the class he is different—you never find out—the kids on the playground will throw looks then rocks—he will cut himself—or not eat for weeks—teachers will not notice or they will be too busy to contact you. So you will shake and pound your fist and swear off prayer. As the door slams again upstairs—the house does nothing but shake now—you will try desperately to remember that Sunday afternoon when he was just two pink lines.

Then, you will wrap your own too short arm and the fist that will not close around the round tight belly of your wife. You will breathe in all of the still dust in your house—the smell of her dirty hair—the pulsing warmth of her back, and exhale sweet nothings. You will give up control. You will believe all prayers are answerable. You will pause and be speechless. Murmur, *My god*

—memorize the infinite wonderments.

Jessica R. Lewis (OPRFHS class of 2001. Original Spoken Word Club member. One-time LTAB member. BFA in writing—Pratt Institute. External affairs manager. Mother of two.)

I Used to Love/P.E.N.S.

You don't
come to me
like you used
to

Partnered phrases
with   rhythmic
ease
Flowing naturally,

in and out
like a moving
chest as lungs
breathe

Now you are an asthmatic wheeze
Mega mucus blocking air path
of what would be

A big breath to make a doctor
pleased after a successful ER test
Using a peak flow

Instead, stanzas and prose
now creep slow in wee
hours of the morning

Waking me
when I should be asleep
Gotta be well rested

Catch Zs to cop dollars
but the still of night
allows a silence that stirs creativity

To scream and holler
alarm clocking
me for my attention

As I'm adulting through
these Mental Olympics
tactics and gimmicks

Moving through a check-
list neglected
the sacred power of pen and pad

As a teen in my troubled times
I wrote rhymes to clear my mind
Doubled in age and left you be-
hind

Like the rapture
unaware putting you on the backburner
would limit my ability to capture

Metaphors, memories, alliteration, and similes
Masked off and passed off
That voice of the people

too focused on downtown high rises
with glass ceilings adorned
with steel steeples

Executive meetings, prepping for presentations,
chummy client lunches, happy
hours, family vacations

I used to love you
Cherished you deeply
Slams were date nights
I kissed the mic
sweetly
Hoped to give you a serious look
Transfer my loose-leaf pages to Word
docs
Make a real commitment
Publish a plethora of chapbooks.
Offer discounted shipment
with an additional purchase of a
CD Perform at the Nuyorican
Be the rebirth of Beatnik
But I pushed you to the
side Kept you as my little
secret
I felt no reason for our existence
We finally outgrew each other
An old hobby, a has-been
But you'd sneak up on me in bars
Sporadic open mics or
subway performers rappin'
Hear you in all kinds of songs
See you daily in motion

I was trying to separate myself
Divide us like quotients
But you're too potent
And though losing you
caused me to suffer
a syndrome of poet's extreme neglect
We're on some makidada
We'll always connect

TACTICS

The question of survival is a tense one. Answers to how people survive, or how people cope with the burden of making through, depend on geography. Our proximity to pain, or anxiety. Our proximity to our beloveds, or the things we love. Some might say that the goal is never simply to survive, but to thrive. I do believe this, of course. But I think what often gets lost is that the road to thriving is paved with several small survivals, each of them worthy of their own celebration.

When I was young, I wasn't nearly as much of an outsider as I made myself out to be. Youth is tricky in this way—there are those who are at the margins of the world, those margins sometimes first understood within the wild forest of youth. I found my way through it all like many of the people around me: I played the sports I was good at, and some I wasn't. I acted in plays, to at least get a chance to step outside of my body and into someone else's. I played music loud in cars, or in headphones, or in bedrooms. And, of course, I wrote. I wrote poorly, with no aim or direction, but I wrote, and I knew that the writing was charting a path to somewhere I needed to be.

For many people who have spent time feeling like an outsider, or feeling like they are constantly figuring out ways to stay afloat, the page can be a refuge. To set your intentions for survival on the page, and then chase after those intentions in the world outside of the page. Or to just keep the moments on a page that remind you of joy, or a happier time. Though, survival isn't always as urgent as I'm making it seem. Sometimes, survival is about getting through a school day you didn't want to get up for. Showing up for friends who you made a promise to. Loving a parent or a family member, even when loving them felt difficult.

That's what this section is all about. Like survival, this section is tender and thoughtful. And yes, it is celebratory, even when it feels heavy. There are odes to difficult nights and beautiful mornings. Poems about makeup and money, poems about cooking food with recipes passed down from the hands of loved ones, poems about the journeys to and from beloved places.

When people speak of survival, my hope is that it isn't just about what scars a person can show, or what pain can be traversed to arrive at something that isn't pain. When people speak of survival, my hope is that what is spoken of are all the small and gentle ways we find to keep ourselves alive. The ancestors who guide us to newer, cleaner places. The resilience we have when things seem impossible.

I am so thankful for the poems in this section. How they uplift and echo.

—**Hanif Abdurraqib**

Charity Strong (OPRFHS class of 2016. AS in psychology—Triton College. College student—University of Illinois-Chicago.)

On Loving Someone You've Learned to Hate

I shoved bullets down my throat
when I turned 17. Prayed
that the last thing to see me
would be my pale ceiling.

That ceiling was my biggest
supporter. Let me paint on it
through my thoughts.
It was so quiet it almost felt like

I could hear someone saying,
"Don't do it." I knew
I hated myself the most
when I didn't listen.

When it became too hard
to live, deadly, I let go.
When death didn't want me
either, I realized how much

life did, how my liver
wanted to protect me
from blood clots, how much
my kidneys wanted to eradicate

my body's filth, how much
my lungs wanted to swallow
air and gift me with oxygen,
how much my heart wanted

to beat, how bad my heart
wanted to just beat for me.
They called me an ocean.
I am not. I am a pond,

the one you see driving down
empty roads of rich homes.
They can't play in me.
They've never heard of me.

But they know I'm there.
There is no sign or plaque
to label who they want me
to be. I am my own. I turn

heads quicker than quarters.
Heal wounds slicker than
bandages. And now I breathe
for more than just me.

Dorothy Moore (OPRFHS class of 2013. One-time LTAB member. BA in educational studies, geography, and urban studies—Macalester College. Second-grade teacher.)

notes on almosts
or, an ode to surviving

truthfully, what i remember most is the water—the black
sheen that engulfed the rocky-bottomed sea each

night i stood & waited for anything. if pressed, i guess there
were also those cliffs, yellow & dry as another

planet. i walked & walked & walked & the sun cooked
me as i climbed. there was that bathroom, little more

than a toilet, in athens, where i threw up & knew i was in
for something much worse, a devastation of sorts,

my body a brilliant & sputtering machine. what did i know
of grief? i woke every morning before the sun did

& stood in the sea—how could i not know it was coming?
how is it that my feet stayed rooted in the water

long after i decided to live?

Le Keja "keja Janae" Dawson (OPRFHS class of 2010. Makeup and hair artist. Owner of a tattoo parlor. Mother of three.)

Get Pretty

Men look at me like a poster board
try to hold me just high enough to be seen
pin my hips to their sides
I must be something to look at but not to be careful with
and men don't care that you're made from paper
They leave small rips in every corner
will write all over you, autograph where it hurts the most

My brother says I just want everything I should be afraid of
That I sign myself up for what I know hurts
He says I need to learn to give myself time
to heal even when the scab is itching
I'm still not sure if I'm built like that
There is no in between with me, no balance,
just the ceiling and the earth and neither have a limit

I learned all my mother's lessons backward
My lips were cherry-stained with accidentally
falling for the wrong one
And when a nigga from the South Side lets love stain
his lips, you listen
You don't question it
It's usually never mentioned, unless you become a casualty,
then everyone wants your portrait on a shirt
I didn't want to die for him to see me
so on accident
I held onto a boy who made me so unfamiliar
I didn't know myself

I've forgotten myself outside the hands of a man
who beats me down without ever making a fist
I been suffocating sharing my air with a man-child
who's still tryna break a woman who broke him before me
I'm still practicing patience for him fighting my mirrors

So I get pretty
Mascara, contour, blush, install weave
Is my pretty enough to put on his poster?
If this is what it feels like to be beautiful
I don't want it
Take the dust from my face
and free me

Corina Robinson (OPRFHS class of 2019. Two-time LTAB member. College student—First Wave program at the University of Wisconsin. Younger sister of Christian Robinson.)

Blood Money

Dear feminine product companies: Do us all a favor and stop
investing in happy girls doing yoga. It's going to take battlefields
of blood for me to show interest in your tampons. No more
flowers, blue silk, or music that really belongs in Barbie commercials.
Give me Walking Dead–level screams of terror. I want the real.
Stop hyping up how thin and discreet your period products are
when the packaging has a Jurassic Park in every crinkle. I want
a company that knows it is every girl's dream to be: a female panda.
The only animal that ovulates for one week, once a year. If bleeding
is our jobs, turning us into pandas is yours. Give me less ways to offend
a classroom when I ask to use the bathroom, while pulling
out a magic wand of cotton and more ways to apologize for that thing
that will happen to every person with a vagina. When the boy in my
class asks how to get a period I tell him it's simple: Put on your
nicest, fanciest underwear and wait for karma to do the rest.
Dear feminine product companies: There is a woman at the
food pantry I volunteer at with five daughters. I have been
sneaking extra tampons into her cart faster than a retreating switch-
blade. My manager scolds me and forgets that he has
daughters, too, and the cost of existing while female doesn't
care about whose bank account it is slurping from. Take my
blood money and make use of it. Fund research that will turn
us into pandas. "That kind" of a woman for only seven days out
of a year. Dear feminine product companies: My mom and I
talk trash about you more than the white boys I go to school with.
She knows everything you have done and has kept an eternal list.
You monetize my body without remorse. Make hypocrites
of yourselves and say it is empathy. I am done paying extra for

my razors, deodorant, lotion, shampoo, conditioner, and your paycheck.
You think reparations come in the color pink and the scent of exotic
fruit. Like your body odor doesn't need just as much help as mine does.
You tax me more for my tampons and less for your condoms.
And don't they end up in the same body part anyway?
Doesn't that body part belong only to me?
You call my body your business plan. Make a trajectory
of nature and all the ways you can manipulate it. As if
women didn't give birth to you. As if
your daughters don't bleed, too.

Christian Robinson (Rich Robbins) (OPRFHS class of 2011. Two-time LTAB member. BA in English and gender and women's studies—First Wave program at the University of Wisconsin. Spoken word educator. Rapper. Musical artist. Music producer. Older brother of Corina Robinson.)

Tamales on Christmas

It is tamale Saturday.
The day the colors of the rainbow break
b r e a d.   Today these Brown hands will be coated
in masa and Mama and memory.

> A family patterned like
> plaid on stripes will go to war with corn
> husks and Grandma Lupe's recipe   h a n d w r i t i n g.
> Today I am not artist. Nor social

media handle. I am not
Black Boy Joy. Nor Brown Boy dead. I am
a b a b y   before its first gulp of tap water. The oldest cousin
still hesitant to clink forks at the adult table.

> Today we pick up the place
> mats Tia and Big Mama and Papa Sisto left
> behind. We've never been the same since   they   d i e d.
> We grew into something stronger

and weaker at the same time,
most ourselves when colors don't
m a t c h   but meat is tender, and masa has no clumps,
and air is clean like a mind

> that has reconciled with its last meal.

Kelly Reuter Raymundo (OPRFHS class of 2010. Two-time LTAB member. BA in English language and literature—Benedictine University. Office manager. Mother of two.)

Monster

Five months and you fit in me like gray skies.
Eight months and my pockets flee the scene.
Nine months—my hospital gown drags against
the ground like roadkill before the eyes roll back.
They hook me up to the machines. My pulse
withstands the torment. I sit still, consent this time,
as the stiletto-size needle seizes into my body.

My toes barely tingle. I am numb. Numb to my emerging
breaths like womanhood. Numb to the half-open curtains
where I am sure my enemies now wish they could peep
with the anonymity of parked cars. Numb to the bouquet
of lilies on the end table and the lowering of the linen-
line bassinet near my soiled bedside.
Numb like before I knew God.

Finally, you are released from me, roaring. They wrap
you like a mummy. I look at my legs, still spread and bent,
I am a monster now. A beast. An alien. Skin pulsates
and pulls and stretches across my abdomen. Crop circles
emerge around my eyes after sleepless nights. My breasts
have become Godzilla's. The ground cannot survive
my shift in weight. White lava erupts. Blood won't stop

shedding beneath me. They move us into quarantine.
The lab medicates to slow my riots. I marvel at the many
wounds I took to bring you here . . .
Even the stampede of friends menacing and armed
chanting for me to *stay pretty*.

The nurse passes you back to me again. I unveil you
from their bondage; hold your fingers in mine.
You are so calm in lieu of the havoc hours before.
It is like you know how hard I fought
so that your cuticles would not become ghosts.

Diamond Sharp (OPRFHS class of 2007. BA in peace and justice—
Wellesley College. MFA in creative writing—Pratt Institute. Journalist.
Editor at Bandcamp.)

Super Sad Black Girl

When I'm tired
I bare my bones.
Swallow my own hair.
Recover from my thoughts.
Drown.
Tweak.
Have a fit of human.
Eat myself whole.
Bleed freely.
Suffocate
gleefully.
Drown.
Bury this
dust.
Amputate my body.
Abandon my mind.
Cry in public.
Want my ugly.
Choke.
Drown.
Tell the truth.
Fall.
Bleed black.
Swim in my own blood.
Stay free.
Wander.
Feel entitled.
Stay Black and die.

Gabriel Townsell (OPRFHS class of 2016. College student—Stanford University. Rapper. Academic all-American wrestler. National champion wrestler. U23 World Team member in freestyle wrestling.)

Street Mythology

I've died every day.
peaceful deaths, mostly.
unspooled insides where respect bonds to dignity,
left this bag of meat and blood
and ignored ambition with tears and jagged edges,
to steam between potholes and 50-cent bags.
the world lends me chalk.
my battlefield smells like playgrounds.

when I say "peaceful,"
I mean that there is no protest.
But until dirt shrouds this lacquered case,
it covers my name,
and there is violence.
bullets in bucket hats, an opus of bucket drums.
it began where they redlined, and
my funeral ends with red tape.

once I've passed on again,
they'll have written all they can write.
the ink won't have dried before my story fades,
there's no room for new history here,
even the truest stories.
less room for new stories,
less still for news stories,
and I am story long before I am man.

last time I died, I was an 18-year-old boy.
the streetlights exposed my muscle fibers,
flesh peeled back gunshot by gunshot, and
the vultures who fired still feast on my memory.
my chains loosened as I lay in my brother's arms,
clutching my stolen fire, arms trembling in shock.
I awoke in new chains, broken by new vultures.

my resurrection is nothing biblical or unordinary.
it will not feel triumphant, and
those who deny me do so intentionally.
I will be one fault from forsaken testimony.
forever more past than present,
a wrinkled scripture.
an Old Testament promise
of wrath before forgiveness.

I always die alone, usually young.
place and time can't be wrong that way.
mug shots fit better than graduation pictures.
gunshots are quicker than court dates.
my legacy—a deflated balloon and airbrush vigil.

Kris Murray (OPRFHS class of 2011. One-time LTAB member. BA in business administration—Bowling Green State University. Police officer.)

Colors Are Heavy

Every morning I see color
purses are squeezed
eyes linger between sips
of sweet caffeine
the gaze of police brings
a syrupy puddle of tension
The expectation of violence wakes
when I do
eats when I eat
and pulls back the grins
of TV anchors on morning news

My daily routine reminds me
of one constant truth
Black is heavy
But just as I was starting to get used to
the weight of my existence
a layer was added
Blue is just as cumbersome
My shirt is new but the weight is eerily similar
I can feel it when my sister asks why
I want to kill Black people
Distance from those that wear
my old color begins to grow

A vest can stop bullets
but is defenseless against
the faint smell

of eggs and bacon
News anchors portray the same recognizable
grins that shift like
chameleons to match the hue
of the next story
Colors are heavy
but I'm slowly getting used to the weight
learning to wear these colors like an armor
trying to prove not all bruises are black or blue

Abigail Govea (OPRFHS class of 2021. Younger sister of Jesus Govea and older sister of Anabel Govea. College student—Middlebury College.)

Why Write?

I write because laughter is not the best medicine.
I used to spew jokes sporadically because I thought it was.
The more I puppeteered my smile
the further I was convinced
my anxiety would peel away like old skin.
Humor was a succulent treat my irrational nerves craved.

There were too many thoughts I wanted to disperse
that couldn't be glazed in giggles.
They crammed in my brain like paper in Dad's file cabinet
never to be seen or read aloud.
So I turned to the unexplored source
I knew comforts my brother.

Euphoria jerked through the grooves of my palms
watching my brother aggressively
write away his emotions and craft perfection.
I wanted to feel the same way.

Fingers clenched the pencil
as my hand synched with the rhythm
of my thoughts thudding against my skull.
Anxiety leaped into the creases of the paper
as confidence skimmed the doubt of writing's benefits
and inscribed the cemented sentence:
It's no joke that poetry is the new best medicine.

Ibrahim Mokhtar (OPRFHS class of 2018. College student—University of Southern California.)

Family Name

Poetry is the lecithin in my life
The emulsifier holding me together
I could be at my house
And still not be home
Cause I was always too Sudanese to be American
Yet too American to be Sudanese
We've always been viewed differently
Whether we were roaming Madison Street or Khartoum
My mom's hijab was her cape and armor
Intu mahbitrafu al hasil shinu mahana
I promise y'all will never understand

> The day we tore our roots
> I lay silently in my mother's lap
> Her eight siblings bellowed at her simultaneously
> As layers of hijab hid the tears
> Cascading down her cheeks
> The day we tore our roots
> I learned that my calluses were ugly to them
> Abraham or E'braheem
> I was neither
> I was family only by name
> The day we tore our roots
> I was in Sudan visiting family
> My dad traveled to see his mom
> Just across town
> A seemingly simple trip
> The day we tore our roots
> My family told my mother

She had no choice but to stay in Sudan
Days of mourning slipped by
The day we tore our roots
I asked my mother why we hadn't said goodbye to anyone
As we started our 6-mile walk to the airport

I remember
Writing *ashar* (poems) till my wrists gave out
Lying on 300 square feet of glossy wood floors
I'd wait on my mom to come home after 12-hour shifts
Blisters on her feet, a fake smile on her face
She'd always tell me
God does everything for a reason
It took years to believe her
But every verse fortified my wrists
And every performance engraved confidence in my ribs
Until I finally embraced the Sudan within

Nicholas Berry (OPRFHS class of 2019. Two-time LTAB member. Visual artist. Taking a gap year. Younger brother of Noelle Berry.)

Mansion of the Figurative

I can make a simile out of a cracked mug handle
say it's like an arm made of sloppy flesh
call it my cousins' clattering car crash,
where the car trips over the rubber of its
feet say it's a nappy head spared from road heat,
the smoldered fumes that form when ignoring
an octagon that calls for screeching
pavement call the handle almost dead

say it's like a relieved smile playing possum underneath my nose
a mug with a twisted arm is still able to identify as a
mug my cousin's forehead, integrating asphalt with its cracks,
is still able to identify as a child's head
wanting to be touched by a mother's lips,
made into something without throbbing

I can make a simile out of a typewriter
call it a tinkling justice,
a muckraker's knife,
say it is ugly like the "boy next door" trope
because the boy next door has been sliding like typewriters do,
slipping out of a womb, and finding his way to my body

call it a monotone scream,
a foster home for unknown paragraphs,
say it is like my best friend,
always moving when I have something to say
call it writer's climax,

the tête-à-tête between metal and paper fibers
say it's forgotten, or better still left behind

for all the similes I can make with the mundane
stretch my mouth into a peninsula,
it will never excuse my pain

a poem will never replace a good night of weeping.
poems exist in order to notice the ache,
give it a new abode laced in verbiage,
a mansion made of the figurative

I wanted the right man to touch me,
touch me wherever my muscles gurgled for air
I considered them a simile for a hammock

twisting around me like a rope burn, a good flame
I wanted to suffocate in the arms of men
windpipe creased into a valley of sweat

I only love men who are adept in leaving
ascended in abandonment of frail things

I can make a simile out of you,
reading this,
staring at these stanzas sideways with skepticism
call you an honest man,
a screaming woman,
a genuine other.
say you are like staring at flame through paper,
revealing your true self with the flick of a candle

you can assume to know my afflictions,
but for all the assumptions we can make about each other,
we can never deny the ache of wanting to be touched,
wanting to be known without having to explain what's wrong.

Allen White (OPRFHS class of 2021. Two-time LTAB member. Filmmaker. College student—University of Southern California.)

Most heroes were written on white paper

Until black pens spawned a new hero on the scene,
he struck down from clouds and vapor.
Lean, mean, wisecrackin' machine fightin' fiends,
his name was Static, victim of police brutality,
but even when he looked beaten and broken,
wasn't another stat in black mortality.
'Cuz he shined like black gold, not a black token.
Black Panther, Black Lightning, Black Manta, Black Light.
Shouldn't have to emphasize the "Dark" in knight
but static taught me that my head was what won the fight,
taught me to look both ways with wrong and right.
Taught me superheroes didn't have to be white
Through his black ink, he still beamed bright.

Savastiana Valle (OPRFHS class of 2017. One-time LTAB member. BS in arts education—Illinois State University. Third-to-eighth-grade art teacher—Chicago Public Schools.)

Diluted

A few weeks ago I forgot who my mother was.
Looked her in the eyes and told her she looked like someone I knew.
It was two in the morning.
I was texting the boyfriend I didn't even know I had,
thought he was a kind stranger who texted me at the perfect time.

I told him I needed a walk,
said not to follow me or I'd call the cops on him.
I thought he was being too kind.
I had no idea what he was trying to save me from.
He came to my house anyways.

I didn't even make it out of my front door when he found me
and I hugged him.
A combination of feeling like I needed to
and wanting to find some kind of comfort.

I forgot everyone that night
and he sat next to me,
as I was puffy-faced and hyperventilating.
Sipping Sleepytime tea in the back extension.
My memory is a bit diluted

and I am petrified for the day I forget I'm a writer.
I used to let poems clot in my IV.
Tried to find a metaphor in every MRI and CT scan.
Hoped that doctors read the poems I was writing in my head, too.
Tell them to let my brain dissolve in a jar full of similes.

I have lost all my muscles to this disease
and I still find soggy pieces of myself,
even on the good days.

The bad ones, too,
where I forget my mother's face,
my home feels like sleepovers at a new friend's house,
and my body becomes the lines of a poem I can't memorize.
To my brain,
my body,
or any part of me that wants to listen,

don't let me forget that I am a writer

because this is the only thing I have found salvageable
because maybe one day I will publish all these poems,
and some girl will read this sodden in her hospital bed
and for just one moment forget about all the life she had to miss,
sedated and monitored,
needles and stethoscopes,
and know that one day all the pieces will come back.

Someday I, too, won't be scatterbrained and numb-legged.
I will be strong and present again,
know when a memory has been rented or gone missing.
Remember what health felt like
on my skin
and in my lungs
and in my teeth.
and know that life won't always be this muggy and watered down.
I won't always be swimming in someone else's backwash.

RC Davis (OPRFHS class of 2022. Three-time LTAB member. National Student Poet of the Midwest—Scholastic and the President's Committee on the Arts & Humanities. College student—Oberlin College.)

Bug Camp. Age Twelve. Mississippi: The Killing Jar

A girl told me how she pinned a beetle.
Placed it in a jar with a poison-curled rag
and split its abdomen, positioning it in a display case.
That night she heard a scratching noise:
the beetle's claws as it tried to scrape itself from its pinpricked coffin.

When I was at camp, I wanted a fire ant sting.
A burning bite to show toughness to the boy
who pretended he was going to shoot me,
the same boy who said that gay people go to hell,
said "queer" in tones that could crack an exoskeleton.
I never was bitten by a fire ant,
but had begun to shed my skin.

My parents had a girl small as a beetle.
A false daughter curling her hand around Daddy's finger,
an insect trying to crawl from the lie of a shell.

> How do I put nonbinary into a jar?
> How do I pin it to the blanket wrapped around me?

I was held in Mom's arms to the sound of cicadas,
buzzed into this world, lightning bugging the sky.
I've always been afraid of death—
a net that can't be avoided,
the crunch of a heavy hiking boot
the space between lying and not saying,
words left floating in killing jars.

Once, when I first began to realize myself,
I tapped secrets into notes on my phone
and hoped that if I died somehow, someone would find what I had written:
unsaid phrases flitting around my corpse.
Because dying with secrets is dying more completely.

At my funeral, these words will buzz around the room:
Sister. Granddaughter. Young woman.
No one will use they/them pronouns in my eulogy.

No one can tell my story the way I can.
Try to put me in a jar, I will always wriggle underneath the lid,
pull myself from pins and flap my brittle wings.

I suppose I've always been flying away.
The drive home from camp,
wanting to run from the car, leaving its metal shell behind me.
Born in the wrong body,
but it's not that simple.

I wonder if I could ever split myself from myself.
My parents thought they had a daughter.
Maybe somewhere she's still here.
She breathes when I breathe,
turns her head along with mine to press our faces to glass.
I wonder if I will be able to one day reach beyond the car door,
to run into the trees and release her from her jar,
watch her scuttle away in the dark.
And leave me there, moon-washed, grinning,
something that doesn't need escaping from.

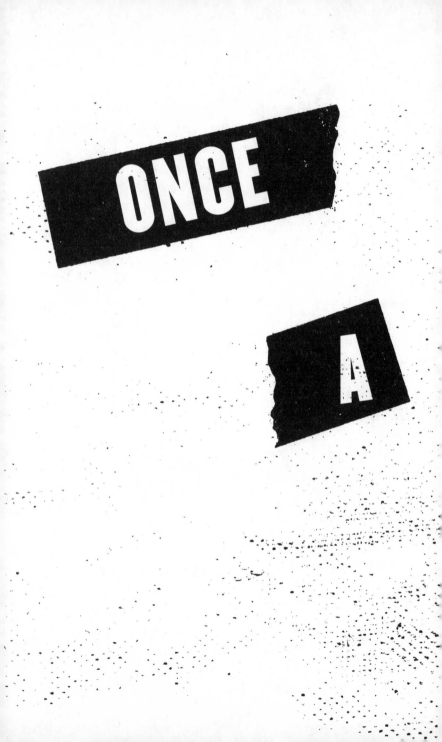

POET

Standing onstage for my final Oak Park & River Forest Spoken Word Club Showcase, I remember looking out at a packed auditorium of family and strangers and thinking that poetry would be my life. Under those lights, I knew that I would someday travel the world as a famous poet, milling over line breaks on sunlit balconies as I'd drink fancy coffee (if my palate ever matured enough to enjoy it). I'd read my poems in packed bookstores as cool kids and tweed professors nodded along and wiped their eyes with gratitude. I would live off of my words, all while somehow making an income that no other poet in history could possibly claim to make. No one could tell me any different: I was going to be a poet. It's also worth noting that I thought I was going to marry my high school sweetheart and walk on to a D1 basketball team. Still, on that stage, I had it all figured out.

It has now been fifteen years since I graduated high school and I'm a little embarrassed to admit that poetry did not become my life. While I did earn an MFA studying poetry at Boston University, I ultimately traded my stanzaed aspirations for telling jokes to drunk hecklers in the back of sticky bars. In truth, I haven't written a poem since presidents were reasonable; also, my then-girlfriend broke up with me shortly after that show and the basketball tryout didn't work in my favor.

I am not the poet, or lover, or athlete that I thought I would be; still, I owe so much of the person I am today to my experiences as a member of the OPRF Spoken Word Club. It is a place that gave me purpose while I drifted between math classes and books I didn't want to read. And it is a community that helped me discover confidence when I otherwise was just a body hiding in oversize clothes. Whether I write another poem again for the rest of my life, Peter Kahn and Dan Sullivan taught me that my voice mattered, and they made me want to give that same feeling to so many others around me.

And that, at its core, is what this book represents. More than just a simple collection of great poems, it is a gathering of those of us who have been inspired. It is a small sampling of the many who have been lucky enough to have our lives activated, even for a moment, by words we didn't know were inside of us. And it is a gift to those who have not yet learned how much their voices matter. This book is a reminder of the powerful work that has been done, and it is a promise of the work to come, not only on the part of Peter and his Spoken Word Club, but the work that so many of these voices are doing in their new communities far beyond the walls of Oak Park.

Not all of us are truly destined to be poets. Some of us are just idiots who tell weird jokes and keep trying to dunk well into our thirties. But every one of us, at some point, has been made to feel whole by what poetry and this collection represents. We were poets for a time, but we are ourselves forever because of it.

—**Langston Kerman**

ACKNOWLEDGMENTS

Many thanks to: Bob McBride, Sue Bridge, Steve Gevinson, Rich Deptuch, Phil Prale, Ted Demos, Cindy Milojevic, Regina Gunn, Jim Geovanes, Susan Johnson, Amy Hill, Karin Sullivan, Dan Cohen, Helen Gallagher, Nate Rouse, Greg Johnson, Joylynn Pruitt-Adams, the OPRFHS English Division (especially Suzanne Allen, Allison Myers, Linda Levine, Sue Donoghue, Paul Noble, Jim Hunter, Jamie Sieck, Brendan Lee, Rich Zabransky, Pat Graham, Pat Staszak, Joanna Garvey, the Belpedios, Nancy McGinnis, Jess Stovall, Avi Lessing, Raquel McGee, Andrew Brown, and Jazmen Moore, for generously volunteering their time) and the OPRFHS Board of Education for the enthusiastic institutional support for our Spoken Word club/program. Malika Booker, Roger Robinson, Jacob Sam-La Rose, Nick Makoha, and Malika's Poetry Kitchen for foundational expertise and inspiration. Spoken Word Club alumni Christina Santana, Langston Kerman, David Gilmer, Sierra Kidd, Milton McKinney, Adam Levin, Christian Robinson, Gianna Baker, Ito Osaigbovo, Asia Calcagno, Grace Fondow, Noelle Berry, Vann Harris, mo Santiago, Isaiah Mākar, and Patrick Chrisp for dedication in assisting the program/club. Steve Young, Don Share, and Ydalmi Noriega from the Poetry Foundation for promoting our work. The Goldsmiths, Concordia, and Roosevelt Spoken Word Education cohorts for embracing the Spoken Word Education movement. Young Chicago Authors/Louder Than a Bomb for additional opportunities for our young people. Jonathan Vaughan, Denrele Ogunwa, Patricia Foster McKenley, Janett Plummer, Be Manzini, Charlie Dark, Dan Cockrill, Shane Solanki, Marty Cook, Miriam Nash, Sundra Lawrence, Indigo Williams, Anthony Joseph, Khadijah Ibrahim, Dorothea Smartt, Zahra

Baker, Kim Ransom, Chuck Perkins, Dennis Kim, Kwame Dawes, Jamila Woods, Fatimah Asghar, Ekere Tallie, Bismark Anobah, Maya Marshall, Debris Stevenson, Inua Ellams, Tara Betts, Amaud Jamaul Johnson, Anna West, Tyehimba Jess, A Van Jordan, Toni Asante Lightfoot, Jessica Disu, Adrian Matejka, Tim Seibles, Rachel Long, Kyle Dargan, Eve Ewing, Marilyn Nelson, Chiyuma Elliot, Gregory Pardlo, Tim Stafford, Marty McConnell, Mick Jenkins, Saba, Ladan Osman, Patricia Frazier, Baron Wormser, Bill Patrick, Patricia Smith, Terrance Hayes, Caleb Femi, Aishling Fahey, Christian Campbell, Kaveh Akbar, Carmen Gimenez Smith, José Olivarez, Sandra Beasley, Aimee Nezhukumatathil, Raych Jackson, Nate Marshall, Krysten Hill, Tanaya Winder, Theresa Lola, Krista Franklin, Dynamic Vibrations, Duriel Harris, avery r. young, Ugochi Nwaogwugwu, and Raymond Antrobus for sharing your poetic wisdom. Carol Jago, Tavi Gevinson, and Naomi Shihab Nye for cheering us on. Bob Boone, Mike Vance, Fahro Malik, Karla Martin, Greg Jacobs, Jon Siskel, Sean Dorgan, Jarrett Frazier, Colin Palombi, DJ Ca$h Era, Lionel Allen, Steve Jackson, Kathryn Gargiulo, Ginger Brent, Peter Quinn, Bernie Heidkamp, Steve Schwartz, Naomi Hildner, Anne Gottlieb, Marlene Spicuzza, the Simons, the Sullivans, the Levins, the Robinsons, Mary Jo Schuler, Mike Bieker, Senator Don Harmon, Phil Hill/Ning, Sam Carson, Andre Moore, Kevin Lampley, Eddie Stokes, Dave Walksler, Don Offermann, Bill Lovaas, Dawn Turner, Dave Schaafsma, Dave Stovall, Bill Ayers, Bill Gerstein, Steve Tozer, Vicki Chou, and Tom Philion for years of support. Timba Smits and Sophie Erb for the cool cover art and design. Hannah Brattesani at The Friedrich Agency for expertise, steady guidance, and bringing us to Penguin Workshop. Nathaniel Tabachnik, Rachel Sonis, and the Penguin Workshop team for breathing this to life. Peter's mom, dad, sister Lara, nephew Griffin, the Sturmers, and the Rogelbergs for their love and cheerleading. The thousands of Spoken Word Club members who are not directly represented in these pages—we hope you're proud of what we've created on your behalf.

Created by Peter Kahn in 1999, the Oak Park and River Forest High School Spoken Word Club is an immersive arts program that integrates students' original poetry into the school culture. Since the club's inception, its members have gone on to win prizes from the likes of the Poetry Society of America, Princeton University, the Academy of American Poets, and Louder Than A Bomb (the largest teen poetry slam in the world). They've been published in *Arts & Letters* and *Poetry* magazine, *The Golden Shovel Anthology: New Poems Honoring Gwendolyn Brooks*, and have been named Student Poet Laureate and National Youth Poet Laureate by both Scholastic Arts and the Library of Congress (two years after Amanda Gorman). On the strength of their poetry, they've earned full tuition college scholarships and a dozen have gone on to earn an MFA in creative writing. They've won Emmys and written with Chris Rock for the Oscars. The program has also been featured in the Siskel and Jacobs award-winning documentary, *Louder Than a Bomb*, and Steve James's docu-series, *America to Me*, and covered in the *Chicago Tribune* by Dawn Turner Trice and Pulitzer Prize winner Mary Schmich.

The Oak Park Model follows the "page before stage" approach, prioritizing the craft of writing. In addition to after-school programming, Peter and an alumni assistant work with 1800 students a year, going into every freshmen English class for two week-long units and every sophomore English class for one week-long unit. During each unit, students read and discuss work by contemporary poets, write three original poems, and read one of their poems aloud. There are in-class poetry slams (no scores shown), semi-finals, and finals (an in-school field trip held in the auditorium) with the superintendent, alumni, and professional poets serving as judges. Guest poets like Christian Campbell, Kaveh Akbar, Carmen Gimenez Smith, José Olivarez, Sandra Beasley, A.Van Jordan, and Patricia Smith are also brought in to lead special writing workshops.

Respect the Mic highlights some of the amazing talent that has emerged from our program. We hope it inspires other school districts to implement our model.

Writing prompts, videos, and other supplemental materials may be found here: www.spokenword.oprfhs.org.

CONTRIBUTOR CREDITS